RECOVER Me

By Yolanda Fraser, LCSW

RECOVER Me © Yolanda Fraser, LCSW

Edited by Julie B Cosgrove www.julliebcosgrove.com

All rights reserved. No part of this publication may be reproduced in any form without prior written permission from the author, who can be reached at yfraser@att.net

Unless otherwise noted, all Scripture quotations in this publication are taken from the New King James version of the Bible, Copyright ©1979, 1980, 1982 Thomas Nelson Publishing.

The views in this book are based upon the author's vast experience as a clinical social worker as well as her upbringing in the belief that Jesus Christ is the Son of the Triune God – Father, Son and Holy Spirit, and who is the Savior, Great Physician to mankind, and forgiver of our sins who extends both grace and mercy upon our confession.

Author photo: Andrew Orr

Cover design: April J McMillan

Back cover design: April J McMillan

Printed in the USA

ISBN: 9798673623084

1. Nonfiction 2. Christianity 3. Self-help 4. Spiritual Growth

This book is full of wisdom. By reading this book, you will discover your true worth and get deep with God about some of those issues you've been hiding for years.

Yolanda Fraser is an amazing author and she is real. Not only does she encourage you to think honestly about yourself, but she writes in a manner which makes you realize that it is okay to be human. This book has dramatically changed my life.

Dr. Patricia Muzingu, Cofounder of Empower Afrika Foundation

Few of us are completely whole. We are complex beings, shaped by our upbringing and life experiences. In this book, Yolanda Fraser shares about her own dark experiences. She helps navigate the reader to a place of recognizing and identifying why they may be experiencing fear, hopelessness, anxiety, depression, trauma so they can heal. RECOVER Me is a great resource for those who desire to be whole in every area of their lives.

Carmela Muratori, CNC

Bad things had always happened to me. I was holding on to the ways in which my life was supposed to be. God answered my prayer and I am now an owner of a flourishing business. I have learned the power of being content when God says, "no or not now" or brings answers in unexpected ways. Now, I am wearing the tangible things of life like a "loose garment".

Brianna, RM Participant

Everyone saw the disaster of my failed marriage. I love the idea of unseen losses that RECOVER Me highlighted. No one saw the loss of status, fading friendships, and my beloved home and neighborhood. RECOVER Me helped me to be seen in my pain not to remain there, but to follow the path that Jesus has for me.

Michele. RM Participant

Dedicated to:

All women who have the
courage to recover from the past
and walk into the future God intends.

Contents

Foreword	5
Introduction	7
Chapter 1 Roles of Attachment	13
Chapter 2 Empathize with Your Experiences	25
Before we move on to Chapter Three….	37
Chapter 3 Come to Your Safe Place	43
Chapter 4 Open Your Heart to New Ways of Being	53
Chapter 5 Voice Your Boundaries	63
Chapter 6 Explore your Purpose	69
Chapter 7 Remember the Power of Hope	77
Acknowledgements	87
Appendix	89

Foreword

*The way through the world
is more difficult to find than the way beyond it.*
--- Wallace Stevens, "Reply to Papini"

This book presumes we are all human. After 37 years of clinical work I have observed how easy it is for any of us to forget we are human. To 'recover' we must first own our humanity. That means respecting our limitations ... and the limitations of others. It means being cautious not to judge others when their lives are exposed to reveal their human nature. And it may also require an appreciation that humans usually heal slowly.

In a culture of "quick fix" and short cuts... our popular mindset may be tested to appreciate how humans heal. Or even how humans get sick in the first place.

It turns out that we, at this moment in time, are learning anew what makes us vulnerable to illness and how healing works. In a time of "social distancing" we are simultaneously experiencing an epidemic of people feeling a need to be connected. We are discovering that a key aspect of what heals is ... relationship.

Imagine. How important our faith can be to teach us about this key ingredient for healing and recovery. A quick survey of scripture punctuates that relationships are not easy. No matter how smart, how wise or how religious we may be – there is still a great deal to learn about ourselves and our relationships with others. In this way, we are all needing recovery.

The author of this critical book helps us walk together toward building an *honest* foundation of owning our humanity and opening our minds to the primary components of our lives (body, soul and spirit) to acquire *relevant* skills that assist healing and recovery. "Honest" means avoiding pretending because someone will judge us. It means finding a resource, like this book, that acknowledges we all have secrets – but also acknowledging that there *are* safe places... and safe people that can help us recover. And "relevant" means the insights must be more than theoretical. We learn best from those who have been wounded and who allow their wounds, with faith, to teach them about recovery and healing. I've always had a hard time learning from someone who seems perfect, smart and somehow unblemished by the wounds of life. The author knows of her humanity, and her wounds.

In building this foundation, Yolanda Fraser accentuates three words commonly used in religious life: body, soul and spirit. Make no mistake, there is a deep and critical background to these components that distinguishes this book from most in the field.

In some ways, redemption is to the Spirit what recovery is for the Soul. For redemption, the Spirit gives hope, lifting us toward better days, and building confidence for the future. And the Soul helps us maintain our direction here and now, in the middle of the storm where the battles are being fought. The Soul sustains us in the midst of trouble and leans heavily on our friends, mentors and peers – feeding us with a sense of home and family.

This book will offer you food for the Soul. It is a manual for an education of the heart… with tools for the here and now, helping you get through the world knowing God is present. Real reflection built into the chapters. We invite you and your loved ones to engage this experience and expect recovery. Then share your recovery with others. I am confident you will find in this timely book an awakening that will blend eternal insights with daily problems leading to a life of recovery for you and those you care about.

Dr. Marcus M. McKinney

Dr. Marcus M. McKinney is a licensed psychotherapist, assistant professor in psychiatry at UCONN School of Medicine and Director of the Day Kimball Healthcare Academy for Community Health in New England.

Introduction

Have you ever felt lost? Not just a little bit lost, but scary lost. The type of lost that leaves you wary of your own instincts. Getting your bearings becomes a frustrating pursuit. You cannot make sense of your current place. You cannot figure out which turn brought you to this unfamiliar location. It seems like you have been going around in a circle, disoriented and confused. You are hesitant about your next move because it may lead you further away from your intended destination.

Should you stop for directions? Would you ask directions from someone you didn't think knew the right way? Can you even trust the directions that you receive? You decide to keep going before nightfall turns your world totally dark.

Lost in A Dark Wood

The great medieval poet, Dante Alighieri, knew what it was like to get caught in a dark place. "In the middle of the journey of our life I came to myself within a dark wood where the straightway was lost. It is a hard thing to speak of, how wild, harsh and impenetrable that wood was, so that thinking of it recreates the fear. It is scarcely less bitter than death: but, in order to tell of the good that I found there, I must tell of the other things I saw there." [1]

Dante's three-part poem, *The Divine Comedy*, captures the raw fear of moving through the unknown parts of life. Dante is clearly describing his own experience. However, with the use of the word "our," he normalizes his trek in a dark wood as a universal part of the human struggle.

We all come to hard places in our lives. We cannot avoid all these dark experiences, so we often try many roads to gain clarity. The dark wood that you may be facing can be a confusing life stage or transition, the loss of a loved one, a traumatic event, or a longing unfulfilled. Dark wood places can disorient our emotional and spiritual insights. These experiences have a way of disconnecting us from God and ourselves.

---

[1] 1. Dante Alighieri *The Divine Comedy* (New York: Random House, 1996), 3-4

Most recently, we have all gone through a collective dark wood experience. The COVID-19 global pandemic suddenly spread over the earth bringing fear and loss. In 2020, this virus has interrupted our very way of living.

I have never lived through a quarantine to prevent the spread of a disease, and perhaps you have not until recently. Thrust into a world of masks, video chats, and cautious interactions, it has been challenging to stay connected to others while remaining socially distant. This has led to mental health challenges for many people. This pandemic has also led to an economic crisis while, particularly in the United States, it has further polarized an already divided nation across political and racial lines.

During times of upheaval, it is good to reflect on your foundation upon which your life is built. Are you building your life on your family, job, or political affiliation? These can be good things, but these can also be erratic and changing as shifting sand. We need a firmer foundation upon which to stand. One of consistency, calm, peace, and love in the stabilizing arms of our Lord.

My Dark Wood Experience

My husband, Gwynmar, and I had a dramatic start to our marriage in 2001. We were married on September 8th, three days before the September 11th attacks on Twin Towers. We departed for our Caribbean honeymoon from the same New York airport that the planes that were used to carry out these acts of devastation. The third day of our sunny celebration was interrupted by Gwynmar's frantic call for me to join him in the hotel lobby. He tried to direct my attention to a live broadcast depicting the horrific news of two planes flying into the World Trade Center. He knew that I'd visited the Twin Towers five months prior.

My first response was to ignore him by slipping into the gift store to buy souvenirs for my loved ones. Surely, whatever it was could wait until after our honeymoon. This was a time for lightness and laughter. Nothing was going to take my joy away from this long-awaited vacation.

As many of us experienced, the events of September 11th could not be ignored. A third plane hit the Pentagon near Washington, D.C., while a fourth plane crashed into a Pennsylvania field. Nearly three thousand people lost their lives that day. Their families and friends would forever be impacted, as would be our nation.

I could not ignore it. It was everywhere.

We called loved ones in Connecticut and the surrounding tri-state area to ensure that they were safe and to let them know that we were safe. Our sadness soon became mixed with a fear of the unknown about our return flight home. We were stranded in the Caribbean for several days since no flights could enter the United States.

A couple of days later, the airlines sent us received new instructions on how to return home. Our travel agent, Juanita, was the best. She worked hard on our behalf. She was a calming guide through our fear.

As we flew home, the fearful quietness existed amongst the passengers. Then a sudden eruption of clapping occurred when we landed. We passengers, thankful for a safe landing, were uncommonly friendly to each other as we taxied to the gate. The moment was filled with well wishes and smiles. I can still hear the extended courtesies such as, "No, you go first," which filled the aisle as we exited that plane.

For more than six months afterward, my nightmares of this traumatic event were mostly filled with haunting images of the smoke and dust-filled New York City skyline. I vividly recall one nightmare when I walked aimlessly around an airport looking for directions and information. I was lost.

I believe that the September 11th attack was a collective dark wood experience for our country. Our world seems smaller, with the increased technology and media coverage. We have twenty-four-hour access to various news and social media outlets. We now live in a world where we can learn of devastation in minutes, whether it happens in France, Israel, or Senegal.

Because we lived so close to New York City, I decided not to get oversaturated with every aspect of this horrible event. I wanted to simply tune it out. However, two years after the tragic turn of events on September 11th, Gwynmar and I found ourselves amid our own personal trek through a dark wood. I realized that getting pregnant was not as easy as I thought it would be. I felt rejected by God. This was the worst feeling for me. I wanted to connect to God and to others, but I did not know how to do it from this sad place. I was becoming a shadow of my former self as I walked through the branches and thorns of infertility. This was the beginning of unseen grief.

Which road would lead to our desired destination of pregnancy? It seemed like I was a walking contradiction. I felt so full of life, yet my body would not produce the life that I'd dreamt about since I was a child. I was the teenager who enjoyed babysitting and worked as a nanny and a preschool teacher during my college years.

Most of my mental health career involved providing therapy to children and families. I was so honored to be a stepmom to my husband's children, who are simply the best. My husband and I became the primary caregivers for one of my stepsons, which I embraced as a timely blessing. I was determined not to allow the barrenness of my situation define my ability to be a good steward of the blessings that I was graciously given.

Hope deferred can break your heart, but hope would not leave me alone.

We still had the desire to further grow our family. The difficult task for me was living in the tension of remaining hopeful while not getting lost in this difficult dilemma.

It was not easy, navigating the monthly losses that I felt in between my menstrual cycles. Disappointment led to progressive anger. This rough patch would soon be over…or would it?

I knew women who did not desire children. Why couldn't I be like them? There is nothing like hope that hurts. It builds you up to believe, but then the crash back to reality is mean. I often felt left out. Isolated in my reactions.

In addition to managing this rollercoaster of emotions, I was managing the barrage of advice from well-meaning friends and family who thought they had the answer to my problems. They knew which direction I should take. I didn't know whether to believe them or not.

How could I not get lost in my dark wood dilemma of confusion, failed medical interventions, and a vision that often clouded as time passed on? It was getting darker and, at times, I felt that I would never get out of the black part of this forest.

Sometimes, I would cry out, "Lord, would you RECOVER Me?"

What About You?

What is your dark place? It may be a different difficult season of life, loss of identity, or loss of a relationship that is shaking you to the core. Losses can be either actual or perceived. *Actual Losses* are typically seen and validated by others, such as the death of a parent.

My struggle with infertility was a perceived loss. *Perceived Losses*, due to their unseen nature, are usually not as easily identified. They can be unfulfilled hopes or changes in our psychological status after a divorce or a job loss.

Both types of losses can cause different grief reactions. Unprocessed grief can develop into unhealthy ways of coping. Regardless of where you are in your journey, this RECOVER Me resource provides a space for exploration and recovery.

Why RECOVER Me?

RECOVER Me is a book that serves as a navigation tool. It is easy to get lost in the hard places in life. RECOVER Me was designed to help you move forward from your dark places in a less disconnected way.

Many women find spiritual and emotional support through RECOVER Me Support Groups, as they heal from their painful places.

However, RECOVER Me is formatted for both individual and group exploration within the RECOVER Me Support Group. Individuals who do not have access to a local RECOVER Me group, can utilize this tool during your personal times of reflection, meditation, and prayer.

Healing is a process, so take as long as you need. Maximize your recovery with the help of a mentor, counselor, friend, or trusted family member. This person can serve as a touchpoint to share your growing awareness or to simply get another perspective.

RECOVER Me has three goals. The first goal is to serve as a self-awareness and reflection tool for your past and present journey experiences. Secondly, RECOVER Me is a practical resource for your body, soul, and spirit as you discover and rediscover wellness skills. The final goal is to serve as a marker through your dark wood experiences honoring God, yourself, and others in healthier ways.

When you choose to let God into your vulnerable places, he brings abundance in many unexpected ways. There is an exchange that happens. He will give you "...beauty for ashes, the oil of joy for mourning. The garment of praise for the spirit of heaviness."

RECOVER Me was formatted to fit you. Here are the things we will be covering over the next seven chapters:

Chapter 1 Roles of Attachment
Chapter 2 Empathizing Experiences
Chapter 3 Come to Your Safe Place
Chapter 4 Open Your Heart to New Ways of Being
Chapter 5 Voice Your Boundaries
Chapter 6 Explore a Sense of Purpose
Chapter 7 Remember the Power of Hope
Appendix - Considerations and Rules for RECOVER ME participants and Group Leaders

There are six components within each of the seven chapters of RECOVER Me._Each chapter contains the following format to fit your process. They exhibit the various ways that we heal and learn.

Words of Life—These are simply the words from Scripture that bring life to the soul.

Attachment Matters—You will explore the quality of your attachments and its impact on our lives. The sense of self and trust are altered when those bonds are bruised or shattered. Which parts of yourself have you learned to protect? Jesus has always been there and lovingly pursuing you. He wants to show you the way through the forest. He wants you to honestly face that fear that comes upon you and to ask the tough questions. His love, once received, redeems it all.

Water for the Soul—There is a story in the first chapter about the woman at the well (John 4). At this well, she comes face to face with her failures and losses. Bound by her female and ethnic statuses, she lived on the edge of life. She was curious and thirsty. Jesus helped to liberate her from this dark wood experience. This section is in honor of her strength received. In this section of each chapter, a resilient person will be highlighted.

Way of the Redeemed — Our faith often grows weary, and our connection is compromised. This disconnection can be seen in our relationship with God, ourselves, and others. Learn practical skills to walk through your dark wood experience.

Welcoming Rest — Jesus said, *"Come to Me, all you who labor and are heavy laden, and I will give you rest."* (Matthew 11:28). We are more creative when living from a place of rest. Increase happens. Focus and enjoy as you learn the benefits of rest and self-care. Sometimes, we are too tired to see a brighter future or to notice and observe the blades of hope springing up. Meditation is an ancient spiritual practice that refreshes the body, mind, and spirit. Zoe is the Greek meaning for the words "abundant life." When we meditate, we renew, and we learn. Stillness brings healing from a place of calm. Jesus came that we may have life and have it more abundantly (John 10:10).

Prayer Matters — Shared experiences can create intimacy in any relationship. This is the place to share your pains, progress, and joy, and to request assistance. You can more easily learn the benefits of gratitude when your heart aches. *There is a science to being thankful.* Prayer can heal unmet expectations. It can give insight into your motives and intentions. Prayer has a way of bringing beauty to your vulnerable places.

Many women have found RECOVER Me to be a helpful spiritual tool to supplement their sessions of professional or pastoral counseling. If you are experiencing life-altering effects from depression, anxiety, or traumatic loss, please seek professional help.

NOTE: RECOVER Me explores difficult themes. Please seek the support of a trusted friend, mentor, or a family member as you journey with us. Or seek out a RECOVER Me group in your area.

Chapter 1 Roles of Attachment

Words of Life

Jesus answered, "Everyone who drinks this water will be thirsty again, but whoever drinks the water I give them will never thirst. Indeed, the water I give them will become in them a spring of water welling up to eternal life." John 4:13-14

Attachment Matters

John Bolby, a British psychologist, was a pioneer in attachment theory. He concluded, "the initial relationship between self and others serves as a blueprint for all future relationships." [2]

As children, we are shaped by the dynamics of our families. The family of origin is the foundation of our development, social interaction, and attachment. When our basic needs of safety, stability, love, and guidance are met, we become adults who choose healthy connections to people. Inconsistencies from our parents or primary caregivers adversely affect us.

For instance, if you grew up with a mother who struggled with chronic depression, you might have interpreted her irritability, exhaustion, and withdrawal as rejection. You might even blame yourself or even develop a pattern of behaviors that seek to get your needs met. Unfortunately, you might have been labeled as attention seeking or aggressive. Your lack of self-awareness may have led to frustration and more rejection from others. Thus, creating an insecure personality.

Therefore, when the family environment in which we grew up, is for the most part, unhealthy, we become adults who lack trust in our relationships. If this response goes unchecked, we can develop unhealthy attachment styles. Personality styles generally form as a result of learned behaviors. If fear, distrust, or hurt dominated our relationships, we probably adjusted our expectations by developing a detached attitude.

---

[2] John Bowlby, *Attachment and Loss. Vol. 1: Attachment* (New York: Basic Books, 1969)

PsychAlive[3] is an online nonprofit resource providing public mental health information. PsychAlive states four descriptions of the four attachment styles as follows:

Secure Personality: People who formed secure attachments in childhood have secure attachment patterns in adulthood. They have a strong sense of themselves, and they desire close associations with others. They basically have a positive view of themselves, their partners, and their relationships. Their lives are balanced. They are both secure in their independence and in their close relationships.

Dismissive Personality: Those who had avoidant attachments in childhood most likely have *dismissive* attachment patterns as adults. These people tend to be loners. They regard relationships and emotions as being relatively unimportant. They are cerebral and often suppress their feelings. Their typical response to conflict and stressful situations is to avoid them by distancing themselves. These people's lives are not balanced because they are inward and isolated and emotionally removed from themselves and others.

Preoccupied Personality: Children who have an ambivalent/anxious attachment often grow up to have a *preoccupied* attachment pattern. As adults, they are self-critical and insecure. They seek approval and reassurance from others, yet this never relieves their self-doubt. In their relationships, deep-seated feelings that they are going to be rejected make them worried and not trusting. This drives them to act clingy and overly dependent with their partner. These people's lives are not balanced either. Their insecurity leaves them turned against themselves and emotionally desperate in their relationships.

Fearful-Avoidant Personality: People who grew up with disorganized attachments often develop *fearful-avoidant* patterns of attachment. Since, as children, they were detached from their feelings during times of trauma, they continue to be somewhat detached from themselves as adults. They still desire relationships and are comfortable in them until the other person wants to be emotionally close. At this point, the feelings that were repressed in childhood begin to resurface and are experienced in the present. The person is no longer in life today but rather, is suddenly re-living an old trauma. These people's lives are not balanced. They do not have a coherent sense of themselves nor do they have a clear connection with others.

---

[3] PsychAlive, What is Your Attachment Style? https://www.psychalive.org/what-is-your-attachment-style/

Can you identify with any part of these attachment personality styles?

Please note that these styles don't have to be permanent. For example, if a person identifies with a disorganized attachment, as described above, they generally will avoid any strong emotions in relationships. This does not mean this person will not experience times of overly dependent behaviors. The complexity of our attachment mixes affects us as we approach intimacy in all types of relationships. If we are not aware or committed to developing a more healthy and secure attachment style, we will then adversely influence our children.

It is a universal part of the human experience to be curious about our families of origin. Many of us share the hope of making peace with the painful or unclear parts of our family experiences. It can be disruptive to our lives today when we rehearse those lingering negative messages about our worth as daughters, sisters, and women.

Let's try to reflect on the ways our childhood experiences are still affecting our lives today. Just imagine yourself with a more secure attachment. What would that look like for you?

You can determine the level of engagement you have with others. Some of you are ready to walk through those early dark wood experiences in a direct and open way, receiving support from others that you trust. You may be like the others who would prefer a gentler entry to this place of exploration. You may want to just focus on the edges of your dark wood experiences. It is essential that we care for ourselves. There is compassion in RECOVER Me for where each person is in their journey.

As one dark wood traveler to another, I confess that I was not always kind to myself. I did not connect to my body as it betrayed me. I did not care for my soul by honoring my grief process. As I grew in self-compassionate, I found it easier to prioritize self-care.

My Attachment Journey

In 1975, my mom was one of two pregnant students in her entire high school. She was "embarrassed" to be a 17-year-old mother. It was a difficult time for both my mom and my dad. She and my equally young father were not mature and could not fully provide for me. For the most part, I was raised in a single-parent home with a great deal of support. What they lacked in experience, my extended family made up for with guidance and assistance. I was the only grandchild on my paternal side until I was an adult. As a result, I was showered with attention from my great grandparents, grandparents, and godparents.

I have early memories of drinking freshly-squeezed orange juice made by my Grandma Mary. I still recall the times I spent after school with my Grandpa Jimmy and Grandma Liz, affectionately called "Mama," until my mom came home from work. This allowed her to pursue a college education. Sometimes, no one was available to provide childcare for me.

She would ride to campus on her blue ten-speed bike with me in the attached yellow child seat. I remember those images of the bike. I am so attached to my mother. Her warmth and resilience are unmatched. The Southern Connecticut State University library was one of my favorite places as a child. I would read and color while my mom studied for hours. I was perceptive and extroverted in nature, or as my mom would say, "too fast."

At the significant age of 10, I began to watch my mom really mature as a young mother with the help of her faith community. She modeled a spiritual approach to facing life challenges. I would hear her praying and meditating on scriptures, which would edify her. She started to develop healthier relationships as a result.

She introduced me to my childhood church, which was a pillar in the community. It served as a haven from the higher crime area by providing summer camps and children's programs. I also felt free to express myself through worshiping there.

Church was my safe place. I took full advantage of this environment of faith. As a child, I would answer the calls to prayer, sometimes with my mother, but often on my own. I would go to the altar to ask for help for whatever worried me. During the times that the sermons would be longer than I could stand, I would daydream and create pictures of my hopes for the future. I would imagine being an actress or a news reporter. I visualized my future, building a family with a caring husband. I would draw pictures on paper or on the back pages of my Bible.

That year I also was baptized with my dad at my childhood church. This shared experience was especially meaningful to me. This would create a special memory to hold on to for years to come. My dad's struggle with substances during my early life left me asking questions. I would look to trusted adults for meaning. Once my aunt elusively said, "Sometimes you must love from a distance." Therefore, I tried to interpret his intermittent absences from that framework. Sometimes it worked, but other times it was an unattainable cliché—to love from a distance. This inconsistency exacerbated my developing preoccupied attachment style. I often would ask my adolescent self, "I know that he loves me, but will he show up for me?" This theme would show up throughout my life, and later I would transfer this question to God.

I am especially grateful for the way that my family discussed his recovery journey. It was not in the context of good or bad. They chose to use less judgmental and kind language such as "well" and "sick" to describe his status at times.

My dad pursued sobriety when I was a twenty-year-old college student. I am thankful for the restoration of my relationship with my dad. It was not always easy for him trying to reconnect with an almost grown daughter. It was thrilling for me that my father was now well. It was also hard to balance my life stage as a young adult as I was ready to explore this new stage of independence. It was not easy for me to trust. I learned the hard way that his journey and sobriety was not for me to worry about. I was just to support his recovery and to live my life.

During this time, I also experienced a renewal with God. I was thirsty for more than a religious experience at church on Sundays. I was seeking a transformative relationship that gave my life purpose and meaning. Could I have a well spring up on the inside of me to quench this longing?

Your Attachment Journey

To start this journey, I invite you to take the Relationship Attachment Style Test. It is a total of 50 questions, and it should take approximately 20 minutes. You can find this test at PsychTests' website https://testyourself.psychtests.com/bin/transfer.

After you finish the test and get your results, you can answer the questions below.

1. What is your initial reaction to your attachment style? Was the result a surprise to you? Write down the experiences that might have contributed to your attachment style?

2. Reflect on your family structure and family dynamics. Where were you born? Where did you grow up? Did you move around often? Who were your caregivers?

3. Describe your relationships with your mother, fathers and/or caregivers. What was your earliest memory of being separated from your parents? How did you respond to these separations?

4. What were your family strengths? What were the deficits of your family? Were you ever terrified or extremely disappointed by your caregivers? What were your physical or emotional reactions? Who did you go to help? How did you cope?

5. Did anyone close to you leave or ever die? How did that loss affect you and your family?

6. In what ways are you resilient? What comes up for you the most when thinking about the reasons that may have led to an attachment style? How does this style affect your current relationships?

7. What was your childhood relationship with religion, faith, or spirituality?

8. What is your biggest concern in taking this RECOVER Me journey?

Water for the Soul

On every journey, you will get thirsty. God provides nourishment for your soul. He can take the hard inquiries and the anger. He had compassion for you as a child and still does today. My prayer for you is that His living water would bring life to those thirsty parts inside of you.

Jesus answered, "...whoever drinks the water I give them will never thirst. Indeed, the water I give them will become in them a spring of water welling up to eternal life." John 4:13-14

Let's see an example of a woman who needed this drink. There is a story in the fourth chapter of John about a Samaritan woman at the well.

The Samaritans were a mixed race. They were universalists in their worship as they not only worshiped Yahweh but embraced foreign gods. They had established the "high places," altars upon which to sacrifice on Mt. Gerizim.

The Jews, who were left behind in the region of Samaria during the Babylonian captivity, had intermarried with non-Jews and were half-breeds, impure. Therefore, as a rule, the Jews avoided contact with Samaritans. And Jewish men would never acknowledge or speak to a foreign woman.

But not Jesus.

This meeting the Samaritan woman had with Jesus was not one of chance, but of a designated intersection. He came to Sychar, the place of Jacob's well. He was tired and thirsty. He sent the disciples into the city to get something to eat.

Could this have been on purpose? Perhaps this lesson was not only for the Samaritan woman, but for the disciples as well. Did He want to be left alone to talk with the woman at the well so as not to subject her to their comments? They needed to break their chains of prejudice, just as much as the woman needed to be set free from her bondage.

Jesus had nothing to draw water with, but he knew someone was coming with a bucket that would help him even though it was noon, a time of day in a desert region when no one came to the well. This was a chore people reserved for the cool of the morning or early evening.

Along comes the Samaritan woman. She knew others would not be there so as not to be the object of ridicule. Jesus asked her for a drink of water. She wondered why this man, a Jew, was asking her for a drink. Didn't he know that he wasn't supposed to talk to a woman of "her kind?"

She had resigned herself to the prison of shame, insecurity, and guilt as a social outcast. But he found value in her, something she had never felt before. Not only did he ask her for a drink of water, he continued to have a conversation with her. This conversation was something that she needed and changed her perspective from the physical into the freedom of spiritual understanding.

He answered her, *"If you had known the gift of God and who it is who said to you, 'Give me some water to drink,' you would have asked him, and he would have given you living water"* (John 4:10).

She noticed that he had nothing with which to draw from the well, then asked, *"Where do you get this 'Living Water'? Certainly, you are not greater than Jacob, our ancestor, are you?"* Jacob, one of the Hebrew patriarchs, had used it for his own livestock more than 1600 years earlier.

Jesus told her that everyone who drank from Jacob's well would become thirsty again. But anyone drinking the Living Water, a living spring, flowing from the very throne of God, would never thirst again. Still thinking only of her immediate needs, she answered, *"Sir, give me this water, so I will not be thirsty or ever have to come here to draw water"* (John 4:15).

He then asked her to go get her husband, but she replied, "I have no husband." Jesus then proceeded to tell her of her five previous husbands, and of the man she currently lived with who was not her husband. She had never encountered anyone like this before.

Like many people when confronted with their sin, she felt uncomfortable. She tried to "change the subject" and direct Jesus' attention off her sin and onto whether one should worship on this mountain or in Jerusalem. His reply leads her back to the true issue. She then asked if he was the Messiah, and he replied, *"I, the one speaking to you, AM he"* (John 4:26).

All Jews and Samaritans were familiar with the name of God, Yahweh, which translates "I AM." Jesus reached back in time to Moses, a prototype of Christ, who had divine authority given to him by the great "I AM" (see Exodus 3:1-16). What excitement she must have felt, realizing she had just had a divine intersection with the long-awaited Messiah!

Upon drinking from this well that would never run dry, she was free! Forgiven! Redeemed! She did not have to feel shame or condemnation.

Just then, the disciples returned from the city. They mumbled, "Why was Jesus talking with this woman?" I can only imagine the looks on their faces, revealing their disgust.

The woman left. She might have been confused by the disciples' reactions, but it was Jesus that made perfect sense to her. She was not ashamed to tell everyone about this man Jesus she had who knew everything about her sins. Her excitement was evidenced by the many townspeople who rushed out to see Messiah, so they too could drink from the Living Well that would never run dry.

Who is the Samaritan woman? Is she your mother, sister, co-worker, or friend? Is she you? The differences between all of us and the Samaritan woman are numerous including that of socioeconomic, educational, and racial statuses. But we can identify with her at some level. Not only do we experience similar emotions of insecurity, anxiety, love, hate, sadness, peace, etc., but we also share the physical realities of fatigue, hunger, and thirst.

What about you? Do you drink from this well? Living water is not limited to salvation, but gives us peace, joy, hope, comfort, and guidance. It quenches our thirst, heals us, and revives us. When was the last time you went to the well to meet Jesus?

Way of the Redeemed

Jesus has compassion for the shameful things in our lives. We do not have to make our abode in those dysfunctional parts. The many failed attempts to heal what we tried to hide still provided protection during our childhood.

Have gratitude for those parts that did the best that they could do for you. There were many ways in which we coped with the pain and loss of the early attachments or various voids in our lives. Sometimes, we dabble in unhealthy coping behaviors that have turned into full-blown addiction. Addiction is a human attachment providing emotional security that often leads to more grief. "There are the classic addictions: drugs, alcohol, food, sex. But we can also be addicted to the rush of adrenaline--it's so tempting to stay wired when the alternative is to slow down enough to feel what is going on within and around us."[4] They result in an emptier and more exhausted state. There is rest as we center on the Well as your focusing point.

Here are three steps to guide you on your RECOVER Me journey.

Step One—*Turn towards the difficult.*
Awareness is like turning the light on to the gravity of your situation. The truths that you ignore do not go away. Denial, suppression, and minimization only work for short periods of time. If you do not see that, you are lost. If you avoid seeing your dark path, you might not ask for help. Your mindset is everything.

Step Two—*Ask for water.*
The woman at the well experienced one of the most loving and progressive interactions in the Bible. She experienced gender, ethnic, and religious discrimination. Her cycle of repression and loss resulted in a profound thirstiness, which was quenched by the compassion Jesus extended to her. I am thankful for the compassion Jesus extended to this resilient woman, and that He provides for all of us today who come to Him for help.

Her dark wood experience of broken attachments was interrupted by the Redeemer asking for a drink. As a result, Jesus offered a better drink that sustained her throughout the rest of her life's journey. When she was bold enough to inquire, she saw that Jesus had a high threshold for her questions. She tolerated the distress of Jesus challenging her long-held beliefs. The well for her was a place of clarity. Her mindset was adjusted.

---

[4] Lauren Van Dernoot Lipsky, Trauma Stewardship (San Francisco, Barrett& Koehler,2009)

Jesus loved her engaged spirit so much that he was also filled. When his disciples came back from their quest to find a meal and offered Jesus some of it, He replied, *"I have food that you do not know of..."* (John 4:32). Hers was an opportunity to seek and to save that which was lost. The reason that He came. It is the same with each of us.

Jesus is God. He can fill the emptiness and ease the pain. His offer still stands. Ask for water.

Step Three—*Imagine a lighted path.*
As you walk down this path, it is sweetly surrounded by butterflies, robins, and the croaks of frogs. A mossy way leads to a creek. You come to a huge rock with a flat surface. Normally, you would not sit alone in the woods, but this space is inviting and calming. You trust that you are safe. As you listen to the sounds of nature, you begin to ponder if you could drink the water that Jesus offers or follow His path of supposed redemption. You begin to reflect on the unreliable and abusive leadership that you have experienced. Maybe you can give Him your distrust and consider trusting again.

Arise from your rock and take the illuminated path that is already prepared for you.

Welcoming Rest

The healing benefits of rest were only learned once I went through my own recovery journey. I define rest as "a freedom from activity and having a peace of mind and spirit." It is a place to rest your mind as well as reconnecting with your body.

This section was prepared for you so you can develop the practice of regular resting in your life. It is especially necessary to rest at this juncture because this opening chapter on family and attachment may have brought up some difficult memories or confirmations of some experienced loss.

This was especially true for me because my relationship with my body was downright neglectful at times. I did not listen to it. I ceased from nurturing it. I believed that I became somewhat disconnected from the body that could not perform or produce what it was designed to do. Oh, the healing that comes when we learn how to love ourselves body, soul, and spirit.

Welcoming Rest is a posture that is crucial to your health and creativity. It is a practice of both proactive and compassionate rest stops that involves reflection.

Proactive Rest means preventative rest. These times of rest are built into the structure of our lives. These can be planned times that some people call a Shabbat, Sabbath, or just a day off. I make a provision to rest regularly so I don't have to be forced to rest due to physical illness and emotional crisis.

Compassionate Rest means responding mindfully. When I face stressful things that cause suffering in me, I choose to respond to this difficult or unforeseen circumstance by resting. I choose to be kind to myself. I choose to nurture in self-compassion. It does not mean I am self-absorbed, but I am practicing good stewardship with what God has given me. I am honoring God, my life, and others by choosing to rest.

I invite you to take a Rest Stop.

I recently experienced a time of reflection. I was meditating on a scripture in Psalms regarding a tree bearing fruit in its season. This time of reflection brought my attention to a tree in the front of my house that seemed to be out of season. Lingering fall leaves dangled from the branches in early January, well past the time of autumn. It seems that we were the only ones in our neighborhood that are picking up leaves as we were hanging the Christmas lights.

At times, we tend to be like that tree. In childhood, we have a perception about how things will be when we grow up in terms of a perfect lifestyle, a perfect mate, and a perfect career. Sometimes our scheduling does not agree with our childhood perception, causing us to doubt the validity of our dreams.

The leaves may be late in falling, but nonetheless they will. What unhealthy patterns do you need to disconnect from now that you are an adult? When as a child, you did what you needed to do based on the limited knowledge and healthy models. Bring some compassion to your younger self but realize it is now time to let them go.

Now, let's anchor our thoughts and relax our bodies. Take a few slow and deep breaths to relax.

We are going to reflect and to practice Proactive Rest. Jesus is offering compassion for your attachment narrative. Try not to judge yourself but notice where you are in terms of rest.

Let's begin to look at your surroundings. Simply notice where you are. If you feel safe, close your eyes, and listen to the sounds around you. You may hear traffic, faint music in the background, or even loud sounds.

Take a deep breath to ground yourself. Bring your hands to your belly. Notice your breathing patterns. As the air moves through your nose, and as it fills up your chest and belly, does the air feel colder or warmer? Repeat this as many times as needed until you feel relaxed muscles and a sense of calmness. As you breathe, say a word of gratitude for your journey.

In these next few moments, you do not have to strive or figure out anything. Try to settle into a comfortable position. Just notice your breath. Breathe all the way down into your stomach. Breathe in slowly through your nose. Notice the rise and fall of your abdomen and lungs. (Repeat).

Every breath holds a different experience. Release any tension you might be holding onto. Let it go as a leaf falling from a tree. Breathe in once more. Don't rush it. Just slowly fill your lungs with air. Now release that breath completely. You may feel yourself beginning to relax. Your breath will dissolve stress.

You can do this anytime or anywhere that you want to relax. You don't have to strive or earn. Just notice your breath.

Stay focused! Your breath is a grounding tool to focus your mind on

Imagine the Redeemer noticing your thirst, knowing that he can fulfill your need. Let go.

Now let your breathing return to a normal rhythm. Notice the release of tension in your body and spirit.

In what ways can you incorporate rest in your life? Maybe a morning or evening routine of Proactive Rest? Can you either designate an hour or even a day of rest? What adjustments to your mindset would need to happen? What small changes in your day, week, or month would be helpful to make rest a priority?

Ask for sustenance as you travel along the way. Even through the abuse and neglect, begin to ask God about the ways He's been present for you.

Share your reflection with a friend who practices self-care. Ask this friend for any feedback for your journey.

Prayer Matters

Let's relieve our burdens to God in prayer. Feel free to add to this prayer or modify it as you are led.

God, I am thankful for_____. I ask for strength as I travel along the way. I have not always sensed your presence with me during my childhood. Help me to receive drink for my thirst from broken, damaged, and unhealthy attachments to family, people, or things. I ask you to bring life to all my dry parts. Bring restoration to any pain that lingers in my body and mind. Reveal yourself to me as a Redeemer of lost things. Help me to see the beauty in my vulnerability. Give me the strength to rest and remain in your presence. Help me to know which way I should take in my personal dark wood experience.

I extend my hands to you. Give me understanding and peace. I pray for unexpected joys to surround me. I ask these things in your name Jesus, Amen.

Chapter 2   Empathize with Your Experiences

Words of Life

Love the LORD your God with all your heart and with all your soul and with all your mind and with all your strength.' The second is this: 'Love your neighbor as yourself.' There is no commandment greater than these." Mark 12:30-31

Attachment Matters

As children, we adjust to our environments. We learn coping skills that protect us. As adults, we are limited by the same childhood-learned coping skills.

For me, not being able to conceive and carry my own child was a huge loss, but I think about the way I learned survival skills from the glorious women in my family. I was fascinated and often bragged about their ability to make lemons out of lemonade. I watched them shake off the pain and live highly productive lives. Loss did not keep them down. I never witnessed any genuine emotional response to a heartbreak of any kind.

The same fascination that I carried for my grandmothers, aunts, and mother was also met with a certain sadness. These beautiful and vibrant women, who were my role models, never allowed pain to have a space in their lives. I am sure that there were social, cultural, or spiritual reasons that encouraged this response. In the mental health field, we call it resilience, which is an ability to recover quickly.

I, too, was not going to let the pain from my infertility make me feel weak. So, I simply buried it in the frenzy of seeking treatments, foster care, and adoption. I thought I could solve my problem of barrenness with activity. I was not giving myself proper care for my soul and body.

Even though I was a spiritual person, I was not one to let others care for me in that way, patterning my stoic elders. I did not know how to truly receive compassion and to be self-compassionate for my plight. I knew I was grieving, but I did not realize the depth of the trauma.

The cumulative impact my lack of self-compassion had on my emotions, and my body was devastating. I became emotionally disconnected to others, and perhaps to God as well.

I then came face to face with the reality of this scripture verse. *"Love the Lord your God with all your heart and with all your soul and with all your mind and with all your strength. The second is this: Love your neighbor as yourself.' There is no commandment greater than these"* (Mark 12:30-31).

How could I love God with all my heart when my heart was broken? How could I love my neighbor when I lacked compassion for myself? These questions led me on a journey in which I learned the power of love in a new dimension.

The thought of loving myself was beautiful, but I was not practicing it. As I began to present my broken heart to God, my love for Him began to increase. He showered me with love. As I slowly began to let Him love *me*, He began to do things that I could not do in my own strength.

As a child, I did not have a close relationship with my natural father, so the concept of God as a father figure was a difficult one for me. He was great for inspirational insight and a mighty source of strength, but I couldn't picture Him as the tender provider for my heart. I had to learn about this aspect of God. As I did, I discovered that our Father God is so kind. He is a gentleman, not pushing His way or will. He wants our love of Him to be a choice.

Out of the abundance of that love, I began to truly have new compassion for myself. I thought I was kind, but I began to realize that my well was empty. My unhealthy attachments to a false sense of strength had drained my inner strength. I started to learn of a new strength that was being birthed out of my weakness. It was the strength of relying upon God, as dichotomous as that sounds.

His love exchange gave me strength to continue my recovery journey. I was for the first time experiencing new births in my barrenness.

The difference between grief and trauma.

Remember, grief can be either actual or perceived. Grief is a normal reaction that is dominated by the feeling of sadness. Trauma is marked by terrifying distress. *All trauma involves grief, but grief may not involve trauma.*

Grief and trauma are similar in that they both begin from a loss of innocence or wholeness. Grief and trauma both involve a perceived, overwhelming event that threatened our connections to others and most importantly to ourselves. In the context to this RECOVER Me journey, we will define both grief and trauma as painful events in need of healing.

The essence of the RECOVER Me journey is learning to receive love and to give love. This love exchange gave me the strength to continue in my recovery journey.

You will learn this as well as when you start your recovery journey from whatever pain has left you emotionally and spiritually barren inside.

Scripture says we are made up of three parts: body, soul, and spirit.

Recovery must include the integration of all three parts of the self. It is the human experience to try to soothe our bodies, our souls, and our spirits. Let's explore the ways that each part plays in our self-worth.

The body is the physical side of a person. It contains the brain. It interfaces with the material world through our senses of sound, taste, touch, smell, and sight. When we suffer prolonged, painful circumstances, we tend to become protective of these parts. In his book, *The Body Keeps the Score*, Bessel Van Der Kolk, M.D. asserts that "emotional pain and disturbing memories can stay in our body long after a traumatic situation has ended. Being able to notice visceral sensations is the very foundation of emotional healing." [5]

I love the acknowledgment of the body being impacted by the "disturbing memories." There has been so much progress made in neuroscience where researchers study how our brains are literally altered by traumatic experiences. Our brains inform and direct our bodily functions. The result is that early trauma survivors are more prone to experience stressful reactions. This stress affects the body. Many of the Adverse Childhood Experiences (ACE) studies make the connection between autoimmune diseases, such as Lupus, with childhood traumas. Other medical conditions that these studies identified were cancer, diabetes, and migraine headaches. The body definitely has an impact on the soul.

The soul is the essence of one's self or the life of a person. It contains the mind and personality. Furthermore, it speaks for the person's will and emotions. The brain and the mind are interconnected for better or for worse, but there is hope.
Dr. Siegel, a UCLA professor, affirms that "the brain and the mind obviously have an intimate relationship, but the mind is different: it is a collection of thoughts, patterns, perceptions, beliefs, memories, and attitudes. The mind can use the brain to perceive itself, and the mind can be used to change the brain."[6]

This made me think of the mind's ability to change the brain. I have more control of the thoughts I focus on. I was so identified with the new life I could not produce, my whole being was affected. I began to heal when I regularly fought for the calmness in my mind. One of my favorite verses for meditation that brought me comfort was Isaiah 26:3. It says, *You keep him in perfect peace whose mind is stayed on you.*

---

[5] .Bessel Van Der Kolk, M.D. The Body Keeps the Score (New York, Penguin Random House,2014)pg?

[6] Big Think, Parag & Ayesha Khanna Does the Brain Control the Mind or the Mind Control the Brain (2010)

The results were remarkable. I magnified the words of the Lord and made a healthy space for my grief. It was like the light entered softly into my dark wood. The warmth of the light is the compassion from Jesus who was leading me to green pastures.

The spirit is the life force that has the capacity to interact with God. Our spirit perceives the unseen senses, such as faith, hope, and love.

Faith is the Rockstar of the group, as it should be. It gives us the vision and direction to believe the seemingly impossible. It keeps moving us forward.

I feel like hope is the smallest of these spiritual senses. It is sort of left aside for the downtrodden. Hope shows up quietly to energize us when we start to lose faith and cannot feel God's love for us. There were times in my struggle to conceive a child that Gwynmar would say to my weary soul, "Honey, I will hold the hope for you."

Love is the grandest of the three virtues, according to 1 Corinthians 13:13. Love is the standard of goodness and patience that makes all of us better people.

The love of God is more than a fleeting sensual feeling. It is an unconditional part of His nature. His love for us is ever-present. This means that it is the substance that transcends all circumstances. It is the very nature of God to love. In fact, I John 4:8 defines God *as* love.

Jesus was full of compassion when he brought healing to others. Jesus always pointed to His Father when He described perfect love. In our Words of Life section, Jesus sums up all the commandments by loving God, and then loving others as yourself.

Researcher, Dr. Kristin Neff, states that there is a proven power in being kind to yourself. She states, "compassion is, by definition, relational. Compassion literally means 'to suffer with,' which implies a basic mutuality in the experience of suffering. The emotion of compassion springs from the recognition that the human experience is imperfect."[7] Whether it was a trauma that has been suffered, witnessed, or known intimately by you, it matters to God.

It is not selfish to acknowledge, turn toward, and ultimately move through this pain.

In our humanity, we want to deny and withdraw from the pain. As humbling as these events of suffering can be, they can unite us as humans. When we develop compassion for our painful experiences, the hurt will diminish over time. The more we resist, the longer our stay in the dark wood will be.

---

[7] Self-Compassion, Embracing Our Common Humanity With Self-Compassion, Dr. Kristin Neff

The spiritual kind of love that God exemplifies through His constant provision of direction is amazing. He is always present through the pain and shame. His love is present at this exact moment in time. It also carries the future promise of healing and the recovery of body, soul, and spirit.

But wait. The shame factor is real. In our attempts to self-soothe and ease the pain, we hide. Shame disconnects us from self and others. Some of us self-medicate through alcohol and substance abuse, over-working, codependency, gambling, sex, or food addiction.

I learned, as a small child, that I could use food for immediate gratification when I needed reassurance. The first memory of this was after my mother and I moved from the safety of my grandparents' home into our own apartment to be closer to the university that my mom attended. This was the high crime area I spoke of earlier.

My mother and I came back early one day from our doctor appointments. To the burglar's surprise, we caught him in the act of nearly wiping us out of our meager possessions.

The assailant had stuffed many of our personal items in pillowcases placed in the middle of our living room. He even had the audacity to eat our food, making himself at home in our home. This attempted robbery became a traumatic memory that burned into my mind. It confirmed my insecurity about being torn away from the sanctuary of my grandparents' house.

My developing brain learned two things that night. First, that the world was not always a safe place. Secondly, that food was a self-soothing tool of choice that worked. I had my first soulish experience with food after the robber left as I took in the texture of French dressing on a bed of lettuce with sliced cucumbers, the tomatoey spaghetti, and scrumptious strawberry cake my mother made that night.

We moved back to our family home shortly after this event. My family provided comfort, but eating was more accessible and controllable. My young self's attempt to feed my fears were effective for a while. But, my unhealthy attachment to food only fed my hunger pains to a point.

My teenage and young adult years were marked by a series of anxious attachment styles and unhealthy relationships until I became aware of God's intentional love for me. That love became so encompassing that it met me in my place of need. It continues to do so.

He calmed my spirit. I learned, well into my adult years, with God's help, to hold compassion for myself - that scared child who did the best she could do. I released the shame.

Water for the Soul

Let's look at two brave women in the Book of Ruth, found in the Old Testament.

Naomi and Ruth were two ordinary women seeking an extraordinary solution to their problems and grief. They came from different backgrounds, distinctive personalities, and diverse religions. Naomi was the mother-in-law, and Ruth, the daughter-in-law.

Their *"designated intersection"* awaited, unbeknownst to them. They slowly saw the value in each other and utilized their friendship to heal. They eventually discovered that the One True God, Yahweh, was the only solution to their problems.

Many years before the two women met, Naomi and her husband Elimelech lived in Bethlehem with their two sons. A famine crippled the land.

This sounds like an oxymoron. Bethlehem means "house of bread." Bethlehem was a place where God's blessings were supposed to flow, a place of spiritual and physical security, but all they experienced was drought, pestilence, and pain. When God's people disobeyed, His judgment was expressed in the famine as a means for them to repent.

Elimelech decided that he must leave Bethlehem with his family and sojourn (temporarily) to Moab, the "land of sin" instead. Elimelech's name means, "my God is King," however, his actions proved that "God was not his King." No mention is made of anyone else accompanying him and his family or leaving Bethlehem, nor is there a mention of him first praying and seeking God's guidance. As the leader of the house, he subjected his family to move to a place that God did not approve, abandoning the blessings of God. His flawed decision affected his family as well as himself. 1

Despite Elimelech's choice, Naomi submitted. She had been satisfied living in Bethlehem. She was now asked to move from a place of security and familiarity to a pagan city, causing her to be isolated from the things she held dear.

This family lived in Moab for ten years. Much happened while living there. Elimelech died not long after arriving in Moab, leaving Naomi to care for herself and their two sons, Mahlon and Kilion. They married Moabite wives, marrying outside their faith. The Moabites served the idols Molech and Chemosh, as well as Baal, Ashtoreth, and fertility gods. To find favor with these false gods, they would often sacrifice their children. This was pure evil. Nevertheless, both sons decided to marry women raised with these practices.

During those years, she never heard her sons say, "you're going to be a grandmother." The sons were not only spiritually bankrupt but physically fragile, the meaning of their names bearing this out: Mahlon meaning "unhealthy or sickly," and Kilion meaning "puny or weak." The sons eventually died, leaving their widowed mother with two childless widows.

But God did not leave Naomi alone.

Hers is a story of God's redeeming grace.

In times of multiple losses, grief can dim our expectations for relief. For Naomi and her daughters-in-law, Ruth and Orpah, the situation had now gone from desperate to hopeless. Naomi was in a personal drought and in need of water for her soul.

Naomi had heard that the LORD showed compassion on His people by reversing the famine and supplying bountiful crops. She decided to return home to Bethlehem. Ruth and Orpah had planned on returning to the land of Judah with her. But Naomi told them that they should return to their own parents. She thanked them for their love, devotion, and kindness they had shown to her and to her deceased sons but encouraged them to find new husbands.

Orpah decided to return to her former home and her old gods. Ruth held on to Naomi, even after Naomi told Ruth that her chances of starting a new life, avoiding hunger, and finding a husband were much better in Moab. She had fulfilled her obligation to Naomi and had done what was expected of her. However, Ruth, who not only met her commitment but went the "extra mile," far beyond what was expected.

She told he mother-in-law, *"Entreat me not to leave you, or to turn back from following after you; For wherever you go, I will go; And wherever you lodge, I will lodge; Your people shall be my people, and your God, my God"* (Ruth 1:16).

Ruth lived up to the true meaning of her name, "friend or companion," and traveled with Naomi to Bethlehem. The whole village was excited about Naomi's arrival, but they saw that a radical change happened to her while living in Moab. No longer a pleasant and light-hearted wife and mother, she had been reduced to a life of misery and hopelessness when her husband and sons all died.

"Can this be Naomi?" they all asked. She replied to them, *"Don't call me Naomi (which means pleasant)! Call me 'Mara' (which means bitter) because the Sovereign One has treated me harshly. I left here full, but the LORD has caused me to return empty-handed..."* (Ruth 1:9-21).

Naomi had suffered multiple losses — the death of her husband and sons, loss of income, and she still saw her Moabite daughter-in-law, Ruth, as a liability rather than the priceless asset she turned out to be. Naomi was tired, worn out, and frightened. Her soul needed refreshing.

Have you ever noticed that Satan always seems to raise his ugly head when we are at our lowest and are spiritually and physically exhausted? He attacks us unmercifully. Naomi thought God was mad at her, so He had dealt with her harshly. Satan had blinded her, not wanting her to see the great blessings God had in store for her. Ruth stepped out in faith, entering unfamiliar territory. She didn't look back. Her courage would bring her to her *"designated intersection."*

Naomi and Ruth arrived in Bethlehem at the beginning of the barley harvest. Ruth went to work, gathering grain left behind by the harvesters so she and Naomi would have bread to eat. The land belonged to Boaz, a wealthy distant relative. Boaz inquired of his servant in charge of the workers, "To who does this young woman belong?" He asked this, not because he had a romantic interest, but he knew the vulnerability of a woman without the protection of a man in that time period.

In our culture today, people typically fall in love first, then marriage. In biblical times, marriages were arranged, and "love" was not the driving force.

Even so, we can see Boaz's genuine concern for Ruth. He was impressed with her character and her love for God, but the Bible mentions nothing romantic in his actions. He was told that she was the daughter-in-law of Naomi, who returned with her from Moab. God, in His infinite wisdom and sovereignty, orchestrated a *"designated intersection"* between Boaz, Ruth, and Naomi.

Boaz gave Ruth instructions for working in the field, and he told the other men servants to leave her alone. Boaz said that he had been told of her unselfishness in leaving her homeland to support her mother-in-law. He commended her, praying God's blessing upon her and that her kindness would be repaid. She thanked him for his reassurance and understanding.

She returned home. Naomi was impressed with how much grain she had gleaned and then asked her where she gathered it that day. When Ruth told her of Boaz, one can almost hear the gears grinding in Naomi's head as she thinks, "Isn't Boaz, as a close relative, legally bound to provide an heir for my dead son? Will he be our source of provision?"

On a side note, both Elimelech and Boaz belonged to the same family, but they demonstrated very different behaviors. When hard times came to Bethlehem, Elimelech fled to Moab, whereas Boaz stayed and endured. Not only did Boaz survive the hard times, but he also prospered! Elimelech didn't prosper. He and his two sons died, leaving three widows to fend for themselves.

Naomi was about to impart on her journey back to "pleasant" after all. She revealed her hand at matchmaking. She gave Ruth the cultural norm on how to propose, and she followed through as instructed. Boaz then recognized that Ruth is submitting herself to his protection as her kinsman-redeemer. She was asking Boaz to be the answer to her and Naomi's prayers.

Boaz took Ruth as his wife, and the townspeople blessed this union. Boaz was established as the kinsman redeemer for the family of Elimelech, preserving the family name.

Ruth and Boaz produced a son, Obed, who became the grandfather of King David. Thus, Ruth and Boaz participated in the lineage of our Redeemer, Jesus Christ! Naomi was no longer remembered as "bitter" but "pleasant" as she became the "grandma" of this new offspring.

This Biblical story is more than an account of a woman marrying a man for survival. It is about a strong woman's courage to navigate a culture that was not always open to outsiders. God had a plan for Ruth.

God is in the restoration business and awaits your *"designated intersection"* **with him.** Like the woman at the well, Naomi and Ruth, we all have a point where Jesus meets us where we are and addresses His love for our needs. When we realize our need to detach ourselves from past hurts, we can embrace God's love for us and attach ourselves to His grace and mercy. Through faith, we have a renewed hope in the One who will never *not* love us, nor will He ever abandon us. That takes courage, and risk. But the reward is amazing for those who try.

Way of the Redeemed

Ruth was strong because she took a risk for connection. She embraced her vulnerability. In her weakness, she became strong by choosing faith. I am sure there was fear in her heart because she had no financial resources or noble status. She could not control her losses and her grief. Instead she took responsibility for her future. Furthermore, she risked it all for a connection to Boaz, her Kinsman-Redeemer. Even in her own complicated grief, Naomi mentored Ruth by pointing her toward her own journey with God.

Jesus, our Redeemer, says, " *Take my yoke (attachment) upon you and learn from me, for I am gentle and lowly in heart, and you will find rest for your soul, for my yoke (attachment) is easy, and my burden is light"* (Matthew 11:29-30).

I was acquainted with Jesus as my Savior. My curiosity grew as I made the decision to get to know Him as my Redeemer.

My thoughts: "This being childless is painful. If only I had tried more medical procedures. Did we do enough?"

Resulting Feelings: Regret, Sadness, and Anger

My thoughts: "When will I have a baby? Will I ever get pregnant? Will I ever be fulfilled without giving birth to a child?"

Resulting Feelings: Fear, Despair, and Disconnection

My thoughts: "I am so tied to this cycle of trying to conceive and the perceived loss associated with it. Giving it up may mean a loss of identity. I do not how to make You my primary attachment."

I began to pray, and the Holy Spirit impressed these words onto my spirit.

Holy Spirit: "*I see you. I am full of compassion. Give to me all that burdens you. I want to relieve and to heal the pain in your body, soul and spirit. I will redeem your loss*".

Me: "I am so tired of going around in circles. I am scared but show me the way."

Holy Spirit: *"My sweet daughter, will you follow me? I am with you every step of the way."*

I initially struggled with this invitation to come to Jesus with my pain that resulted from tirelessly trying to conceive. What would it mean to let go of the anxious attachment to this elusive baby? What would receiving rest for my weary soul look like? These were questions that I pondered in my heart and shared with my husband, Gwynmar.

For sure, grief can be messy and unpredictable. There is no specific time frame. I got lost in my grief. I did not know how to receive this compassion from the Redeemer. Embracing self-compassion seemed like a cop out. Self-criticism seemed like a more familiar companion.

Welcoming Rest

(Before we begin, please get a cup of drinking water to sip as we go through this exercise.)

Sometimes the experiences in the dark wood may disconnect you from your own self-awareness. Take a moment to picture yourself receiving more love. What does that "receiving more love" look like to you?

Like a child, let your imagination flow. What colors do you see as you picture yourself partaking of this love? What sounds of love do you hear? What opposing thoughts will come up as you imagine more love in your life? Gently return to your image of love knowing that opposing thoughts will come; it is part of the human experience. However, you can choose to meditate on lovely things.

Now, sit or lie down in any position that is comfortable to you. Touch or hold any place on your body that feels comforting to you.

Take a deep breath, and then another cleansing breath. With each breath, allow yourself to get closer to that Life that is already in you.

With each breath, be mindful of your connection to your body at this very moment. Notice the way the air causes your chest to rise. Allow yourself to become more relaxed.

Repeat these affirmations verbally of compassion between breaths:

I am worthy of love.

I can receive love.
I can receive freedom from my experiences in dark wood.
I empathize with my experiences.
I am worthy of love.
I can receive love.
I allow this love to flow just as it is.
I am self-compassionate.
I am compassionate to others.
My dark wood experience did not kill my ability to receive.
I receive all things ordained for me.
I reject self-destructive thoughts.
I welcome thoughts of compassion.
I give space to my body for all that it endured.
I hold space for self-compassion, for my soul in need of water.
I honor my spirit for connecting me to the Source of all life.
I am learning to embrace with kindness my body, my soul, and my spirit.

Take a few gentle breaths.
Extend gratitude for your participation with this guided meditation. Drink some water to close out this meditation. Don't hurry off. Take all the time that you need to reflect on receiving compassion from Jesus and developing self-compassion.

Every time I allow myself to come to a place of the warm acknowledgment of my suffering, I am making progress. The rough terrain of unfulfilled expectations can bring about a quiet shame. Every time that I can sit a little bit longer with my lived experience, not to re-live or re-hash the details, but to extract the goodness, the more shame is dispelled in the warmth of the light and the life that water brings.

Prayer Matters

Lord, in this moment, I am thankful for _____. I ask for strength as I become more familiar with compassion. Help me to receive the Redeemer's love and grace towards me. I struggle at times to feel worthy of such extravagant love. I ask You to heal me from broken, damaged, and unhealthy attachments to family, people, or things. Bring healing to my painful experiences. Redeem my shame that I may hold in my body, my soul, and my spirit. Help me to see the beauty in my vulnerability. Help me when I fall. I need Your strength to choose the path of perfect love vs. fear. I don't know what that looks like for me, but I know that I need Your peace in my life. You can provide nourishment for my body, soul, and spirit. I receive grace for myself. Help me to extend grace and loving-kindness to others. I ask that You heal the brokenhearted today. Help me to notice my progress. I pray for unexpected joys to surround me. I ask these things in Your name, Jesus, Amen.

Notes:

Before we move on to Chapter Three....

So where in the world are you?

You may be in a hard place of isolation due to shame. I extend loving kindness for all of your lived experiences. As we gently turn toward the difficult, the path becomes clearer when compassion begins to permeate the hard places. Remember that you can take breaks and go at a pace that feels safe for you.

I ask that you find your Adverse Childhood Experience (ACE) score. It measures for 10 types of childhood trauma in the ACE Study. These include severe family impairment, child abuse and neglect. There are many additional types of childhood trauma, such as, witnessing family violence, homelessness, and racism. The ACE Study included only those 10 childhood traumatic events that were most often mentioned by the 300 group participants. If you would like to explore more about the Adverse Childhood Experiences, visit the Center for Disease Control and Prevention at https://www.cdc.gov.

Remember if you are not ready to dive in at this juncture, there is compassion for you. We will meet you in Chapter Three. But we hope at some point your return to this section.

Adverse Childhood Experience (ACE)

1. Before your 18th birthday, did a parent or other adult in the household often or very often...swear at you, insult you, put you down, or humiliate you? *or* act in a way that made you afraid that you might be physically hurt?

2. Before your 18th birthday, did a parent or other adult in the household often or very often...push, grab, slap, or throw something at you? *or* ever hit you so hard that you had marks or were injured?

3. Before your 18th birthday, did an adult or person at least five years older than you ever...touch or fondle you or have you touch their body in a sexual way? *Or* attempt or actually have oral, anal, or vaginal intercourse with you?

4. Before your eighteenth birthday, did you often or very often feel that…no one in your family loved you or thought you were important or special? *Or* your family didn't look out for each other, feel close to each other, or support each other?

5. Before your 18th birthday, did you often or very often feel that…you didn't have enough to eat, had to wear dirty clothes, and had no one to protect you? *Or* your parents were too drunk or high to take care of you or take you to the doctor if you needed it?

6. Before your 18th birthday, was a biological parent ever lost to you through divorce, abandonment, or other reason?

7. Before your 18th birthday, was your mother or stepmother: often or very often pushed, grabbed, slapped, or had something thrown at her? *Or* sometimes, often, or very often kicked, bitten, hit with a fist, or hit with something hard? *Or* ever repeatedly hit over at least a few minutes or threatened with a gun or knife?

8. Before your 18th birthday, did you live with anyone who was a problem drinker or alcoholic, or who used street drugs or abused prescription drugs?

9. Before your 18th birthday, was a household member depressed or mentally ill, or did a household member attempt suicide?

10. Before your 18th birthday, did a household member go to prison?

How to Score:

Add one point for each type of painful experience. Basically, the higher your ACE score, the higher your risk of health and mental health issues.

Dr. Stephen Porges, Professor of Psychiatry at the University of North Carolina, created the Traumatic Stress Research Consortium. He stated that "research confirmed that higher ACE scores (exposure to a greater number of adverse experiences) were related to longevity and virtually every major medical disorder including heart disease, stroke, Alzheimer's, cancer and diabetes. More recent evaluations have linked ACE to increased risk for suicide, addiction, and psychiatric disorders ranging from attention deficit disorder to psychoses."[8]

---

[8] The Guardian, Stephen Porges: 'Survivors are blamed because they don't fight' Andrew Anthony (2019)

His theory details the trauma survivors' "inability to move, the numbness of the body and functionally disappearing. Survivors are shamed and blamed because they didn't mobilize, fight and make an effort. That's a misunderstanding. It's a poorly informed explanation because the body goes into that state and they can't move." [7]

Oh, the levels of intense shame that even children experience. I hear this shame in many of my adult clients, as they described the blame that others projected on them. It is even more tragic when they blame their four or five-year-old selves for not fighting back their childhood abuser.

The path to healing is opened when we can develop empathy and compassion for all that we have experienced. Jesus was full of compassion when he brought healing to others during His earthly ministry. This same compassion is available to you right now.

Reflection Questions -

1. Is there a part(s) of your body that you have strong feelings of shame or rejection? Name the strong emotions that feel trapped within your body? In what healthy and unhealthy ways, did you try to soothe your body?
2. What memories do you hold closely? Did certain attitudes or beliefs develop as a result of your painful childhood or adult experiences?
3. Have you ever felt that God was not present during your darkest experiences? What beliefs have you developed about God and yourself?
4. What ideas do you hold about being self-compassionate? Name one way that you can begin empathizing with your experience.

I invite you to stop and rest. This is a simple grounding technique. As you continue to read, pause, and take your time as you move through this exercise. It can be done anytime that you are experiencing overwhelming emotions.

Hold on to something comfortable like a pillow, a blanket, or a stuffed animal. Imagine that you are in a safe place. Feel the safety of that familiar place.

Know that you are welcome in this place.

Breathe in slowly and steadily from the core of your body.

Breathe out tension and fear.

Repeat the process of breathing in slowly and breathing out stress.

If further grounding is needed, write three things that you are grateful for in this moment.

Before we move on to the next steps, let's review the steps from Chapter 1.

1. *Turn towards the difficult* — I began to assess my situation and my location in life. I began to really take an honest look at the damage that infertility had caused. I wrote in my journal the truth about my pain. Awareness is like turning the light on to the gravity of your situation. Denial, suppression, and minimization worked for a short time. I was lost in my dark wood. I developed a pattern of disconnection in my body. I was not being kind to my body by providing it with appropriate care. I was not practicing the right amount of mental rest. Denying the magnitude of my pain was no longer an option for me.
2. *Ask for water* — I was in thirst. I needed a drink. I needed direction. It was the most vulnerable I'd been in my life. It was quite beautiful to be broken and to be present. Oh, that Jesus was mindful of me. I was turning toward Him at my personal well. I was tired from grieving over lost things and I needed to heal. I asked for a drink of water not only from the Savior, but from my Redeemer.
3. *Imagine a lighted path* — As I imagined a lighted path, I became inspired to decide to trust. I arose from my rock of disillusionment. My path was illuminated and prepared by my Redeemer.

We all have dreams, relationships, and situations that we expected for our lives. Let us bring empathy to those empty spaces. Now, let's consider the next three steps for our journey.

4. *Turn towards self-compassion* — Trust and kindness are virtues of self-compassion. Self-compassion offers healing to oneself by becoming aware of your pain and turning towards the difficult. Self-indulgence numbs and denies your pain.

    A. **Acknowledge the pain.** In what ways has the pain affected your body or health? Do you have muscle tension, difficulty sleeping or headaches? Stress can also be seen through the worsening of an existing health problem. Some stress can manifest with either emotional or behavioral symptoms. These may include feeling rejected, depressed, angry, or not functioning as well at work or school. Are you having more disagreements with family and loved ones?

B. **Extend some grace to yourself**. Self-compassion allows us to handle our humanness. Are your thoughts about yourself negative or overly critical? Maybe you needed to be overly

Notes:

Notes:

Chapter 3   Come to Your Safe Place

Words of Life

The L*ORD* *is my shepherd, I lack nothing.*
² He makes me lie down in green pastures,
he leads me beside quiet waters,
³ he refreshes my soul.
He guides me along the right paths
for his name's sake.
⁴ Even though I walk
through the darkest valley,
I will fear no evil,
for you are with me;   Psalm 23:1-4

Attachment Matters

Have you ever had a dream, a goal, or a plan that has become tangled in the briars of disappointment? Most of us have. Perhaps we didn't get that pony we wanted for Christmas when we were five. Or we didn't snag that guy in junior high who decided to date our nemesis instead. Or we were not picked for the band in high school, nor did we get into the college that was our first choice. We were passed up for that promotion. We never entered the mission field. We never wrote that bestselling book. Mr. Right ended up being oh, so wrong. We never had kids...

Disillusionment settles into our hearts and we stare in the mirror as we brush our teeth and whisper, "What's the point?" Why try anymore? Nothing seems to go our way. We must have been born under a rain cloud instead of a silver lining. Welcome to the pity party.

Voids are uncomfortable, so we try to fill them anyway we can. Perhaps by eating comfort foods, or doing drugs or drinking alcohol, or even exercising until we drop to the pavement gasping for breath as our hearts pound in our chests. Or we become workaholics and pile on the stress so we can prove to ourselves we can conquer it.

Maybe we cut ourselves because that pain sort of feels good. It means we are alive. Perhaps we find casual sexual partners or entanglements who can please us and help us forget the pain, if just for a few minutes. We can control their reactions. We feel desirable, so that boosts our ego.

"These are classic addictions: drugs, alcohol, food, sex. But we can also be addicted to the rush of adrenaline. It's tempting to stay wired when the alternative is to slow down enough to feel what is going on within and around us." [9]

I once filled my voids through work, serving others in ministry and food. Then, as I embraced Jesus as my Redeemer, I was beginning to grow in self-compassion. During one of my rest stops, the Holy Spirit internally asked me these three questions.

Holy Spirit: "What do you want?"
Me: "A baby."
Holy Spirit: "What are your motives?"
Me: "I want to have a baby because that was always the plan. Come on; it's a natural desire. Do you ask every woman who wants to be a mother this question? Okay, I'm sorry, but this feels like I am being punished. Just tell me what I need to do, and I'll do it."
Holy Spirit: "Will you follow me? I see you. I will redeem your loss."
Me: "I thought I was."

This dialogue left me perplexed. My burden was heavy and had begun to take its toll on me physically. The emotional injuries I absorbed were too significant to ignore. I knew I could not go on any further in the darkness.

I was at a crossroad in the forest. Which road should I take? Should I just retreat in failure? Or...should I take Jesus up on his offer to redeem my loss?

I have been in church most of my life. I heard it said that Jesus is a Redeemer, but to be honest, I did not know what this meant. It was unfamiliar to me.

One thing I was familiar with — my burden. I began to over-identify with it. Someone would ask me, "Do you have children?" My response was, "Yes, I have amazing stepchildren, but I don't have any natural children." I felt I had to clarify. I knew my response was intensely weird, not because of my answer but because of my shame. I could not contain it and could not go on like this, feeling so lost in my dark wood.

---

[9] .Laura van Dernoot Lipsky, Trauma Stewardship (San Francisco, Barrett-Koehler,2009)109

At this point, I was married ten years. I did not know what to believe. In my vulnerability, I began to ask Jesus to show me through this dark wood section of overgrown grief.

My curiosity about Jesus, the Redeemer, increased. In Rio de Janeiro, Brazil, near the Atlantic coast, stands one of the "New Seven Wonders of the World." The Christ the Redeemer statue was dedicated in 1931 as a symbol of peace. It was designed by engineer Heitor da Silva Costa and created in France by sculptor Paul Landowski.

It took nine years to construct. It is covered with six million stone tiles. It is made of steel and coated in soapstone. Corcovado Mountain, where this remarkable statue of Jesus with outstretched arms overlooking Rio de Janeiro now stands atop, was previously surrounded by thick forest. It was not until 1824 that the path was opened to reach its summit. In 2004, escalators and elevators were installed to make it more accessible. Previously one would have the option to take a small train up Corcovado Mountain as well as trek up 200 steps to the statue. There is also the option of hiking up the mountain, which takes about an hour. On this well-worn trail, no one can get lost.

Think about that for a moment. Jesus helps us find the way to Him. No one gets lost. That is what redemption means.

But before Christ came to earth, the Hebrew people were lost. As it says in Jeremiah 50:6, *"My people have been lost sheep; their shepherds have led them astray and caused them to roam on the mountains. They wandered over mountain and hill and forgot their own resting place."*

They searched for a Messiah, not realizing He would soon stand in their midst. Their focus on their plights of being conquered and controlled by foreign powers again and again blinded them. Their own imagined ideas of what their Redeemer would be— a strong soldier-king to save them from the evil Romans— distorted their faith.

Come to Your Safe Space, A Grounding Tool

You can bow in a prayer posture or sit comfortably. Focus on how your body feels. Notice the way your body parts feel from head to toe. Can you feel the texture of your hair on your face? Do your shoulders feel loose or stiff? Rest your attention on your hands. Press them into the fabric of your clothing or a nearby chair or bed. Look at each finger. Slowly move your fingers. Open your hands. Rest them there. What are they carrying this morning? It may be a faint concern or an intense worry. God has a plan for things that concern you. He is waiting for you to place those fears in His hands. "The LORD watches over you-- the LORD is your shade at your right hand. This implies that He is your protection. He wants to be that safe place for you. Let Him care for and direct you.

Water for The Soul

In the book of Luke, Chapter 15, Jesus tells of how He has come to find the lost sheep. It says He, as the Good Shepherd, will leave the ninety-nine other sheep to go in search for the lost one. He then tells two more parables about seeking the lost.

The next one is about a woman who lost a coin and searched high and low until she found it. She never threw up her hands and gave up.

Finally, He tells the story of a lost son. The story is often known as the Prodigal Son, but it is more about the redemptive father, who represented our Father in Heaven. The boy demanded his inheritance, and the father gave it to him. He left the family farm and enjoyed a self-indulgent lifestyle in the city. He made wrong choices to ease the pain he felt, though we are not sure what it was. Perhaps it was not being the first born or he may have simply been lonely for the life he chose to leave behind. Anyway, his money ran out, and he ended up stealing food from the slop thrown to the pigs. Note that pigs were seen as dirty, defiled animals to the Hebrews. So, this young man sunk to the most disgusting image his upbringing could imagine.

He crawled home on his hands and knees, fully expecting his father to make him work to pay him back. Instead, the father welcomed him with open arms. He redeemed the son from his shame and restored their relationship.

Jesus is our Redeemer. He seeks out the lost and restores the despondent. But how often do we cower when we hear His voice calling us? Shame and guilt over the unhealthy emotional attachments we have made make us want to hide.

I knew I was one of those lost sheep, tangled in the brambles of disappointment and failure deep in my dark wood. The more I struggled, the more stuck I became. The loss of innocence and the hard work of shame to keep it hidden or protected. A certain closeness to my husband. A joy for life. A positive outlook on my future. Could my life be complete even without the fulfillment of my desire? My husband is my strongest encourager, and he would just hold me.

After I recognized the attachments in my life and empathized with my experiences, I was able to notice the ways I was being cared for in my grief. Being cared for in my grief was something I really did take for granted. It was essential to my healing to learn that I had a previous anxious attachment style to understand the reasons that I sometimes struggled with the gift of being cared for especially, at this time.

Gwynmar is phenomenal, and he is a loving partner, but the care from the Lord is something special. His loving kindness was transformative. Before I received his care for me, I was generally thankful, but with a preoccupied gratefulness. I was so focused on my goal of conceiving and giving birth to a child; I struggled to hear the Shepherd's voice in this matter.
I really could not hear Him as in the years past when I had experienced knowing His voice. This called for a different type of rest—a proactive rest.

The structure that works for me may not be helpful for you, but you must start somewhere.

Before I would start the day, I would reflect on The Lord's Prayer before I left my bed. I would not do it as a perfunctory task, but as a framework to posture myself--it was my preventative grounding tool. It was my act of morning worship. I would then typically turn towards the Abide Meditation for a guided meditation which you can explore online at the website https://abide.co/ or download the app.

I would spend designated time in the mornings praying for others and then journal writing. The evenings were more for study of the bible and meditation on the bible. The focus of this time is quality, not quantity. The blessing is in the start.

Matthew 6:9-13 - New King James Version (NKJV) The Lord's Prayer

In this manner, therefore, pray:
Our Father in heaven, Hallowed be Your name.
Your kingdom come.
Your will be done
On earth as it is in heaven.
Give us this day our daily bread.
And forgive us our debts,
As we forgive our debtors.
And do not lead us into temptation
But deliver us from the evil one.
For Yours is the kingdom and the power and the glory forever. Amen.

There are so many voices that tried to compete for my attention, especially when I was in pain. Instead of fearing the words in that prayer, "Your will be done" I slowly began to embrace them.

I noticed the Shepherd leading me beside the quiet waters. The challenge was to pay attention and to seek out his voice more than any other voice. The Lord is my shepherd and my safe place.

Learning how to sit in the stillness of His care was a treasure. The Lord is my shepherd, I shall not want. I lack nothing.

I began the quiet practice of coming to my safe place. Practice sitting still, not wanting anything but just focusing on the things that I have instead of those I did not have. Before I could move forward, I had to practice sitting with the painful feelings and then submitting this pain to God.

What desire has interfered with your hearing the Shepherd's voice? What makes His presence a safe place? We can honestly communicate our unfiltered feelings to Him. Feelings of loss, anger, and loneliness are welcome in His presence.

"Ignoring our emotions is turning our back on reality, listening to our emotions ushers us into reality. And reality is where we meet God... Emotions are the language of the soul. They are the cry that gives the heart a voice... However, we often turn a deaf ear — through emotional denial, distortion, or disengagement."[10]

Join me in this hearing exercise as you pay attention to your loss. Replace my desire for a child with your desire and reflect on your experiences.

1. The voice of entitlement that tries to persuade you of your goodness. "You deserve a child because there are so many bad people that have children. You are not like them. You would cherish a child."

2. Then there is a voice of confusion that defiantly declares that "I just need clarity. I need understanding. God has not given me knowledge about the reason that I don't have a child."

3. Finally, there is what I like to call the new voice. This is the most deceptive of them all, it states if only I make a new move, then I will position myself to receive all of my dreams.

I also found His presence to be safe because there is no criticism for the place that I was in at the moment. I kept going around the mountain with my grief. I would share my heart in prayer, and I found acceptance. The Holy Spirit, in His still small voice, would nudge me and teach me. He would take away my silent bitterness and lessen my sorrow.

My soul grew stronger. My spirit became renewed. The greatest treasure that I obtained in His presence was contentment. The exchange of wanting something for wanting nothing but the will of God for my life was a process. My desire for a child did not go away, but it was no longer a burden for me to produce with efforts of praying, fasting, and being good for Jesus. I was now wearing my hopes as a loose garment.

---

[10] .Peter Scazzero, Emotionally Healthy Spirituality: Unleash a Revolution in Your Life In Christ, Thomas Nelson Inc,2011

I was having lunch with a friend. She began to inquire about my position with the "whole baby stuff. "To my surprise, I blurted the words," I don't know if I still want a child."
Of course, one loses hope in expecting something for years that does not manifest. I had been there before, but a despondent spirit was not behind my shocking response. I was facing my ultimate fear. I was no longer suffocated by the thought of living fully without my desire if that was not the will of God for me. I was turning towards the loss of having those shared experiences and joy of pregnancy and childbirth with my husband. Of not being called "Mommy" and God was healing me.

In the stillness, I would hear His voice. "Yolanda, do you believe that I can redeem this situation?" I did not fully know what "redeemed" meant for me, but I was content with the Lord as my Shepherd. I was curious to find out.

Way of the Redeemed

My church upbringing told me that one day believers would be saved. This was not our home and suffering in this world is normal. But we have redemption in heaven. Look to the future when we will be walking the streets of gold, no more sorrow, no more pain. We sang hymns about that with gusto.

But what about now? Today, when we are hurting. Are we to ignore this? We get attached to the idea forever— the Eternal. But it is necessary to grieve each loss. When Jesus detaches us from the brambles, like a shepherd does a lost and injured sheep, does he not tend to our wounds? Is He not the Great Physician?

Jesus healed the sick when He walked the earth. He still does. We can see Him as our Redeemer, allowing others to see the change in our lives. He brings healing to our wounded hearts.

An old hymn says,

> There is a balm in Gilead
> to make the wounded whole.
> There is a balm in Gilead
> to heal the sin-sick soul.

> 1. Sometimes I feel discouraged,
> and think my work's in vain,
> but then the Holy Spirit
> revives my soul again.

2. Don't ever feel discouraged,
for Jesus is your friend,
who, if you ask for knowledge,
will never fail to lend.

3. If you cannot preach like Peter,
if you cannot pray like Paul,
you can tell the love of Jesus,
who died to save us all.

Many believe it is taken from a poem by John Newton in 1779, who wrote many hymns. He opens the poem with:

How lost was my condition
Till Jesus made me whole!
There is but one Physician
Can cure a sin–sick soul.

I began to learn to let Jesus free me from my unhealthy attachments, untangling the dark wood briars one by one. It was not in the way that I thought it could happen. I was learning that His way was better. It was a struggle at times to live as a daughter redeemed, but it was worth it.

The woman at the well had unhealthy attachments, as we have seen. Jesus offered her Living Water to heal her sins and the wounds they had caused. Water can cleanse wounds and help them to heal faster. The water washed out the bacteria that can fester.

Jesus brings that healing water to the lost, like us. I began to enjoy the benefits of turning towards the difficult, asking for water and looking for the lighted path. I was becoming more self-compassionate, and this led me to my next and only step for this chapter.

Bring some awareness to any positive or supportive connection in your life. It may be from your past or present. It may be an internal or external resource, such as, a strong sense of self-worth or stable friend that keeps your sane. Do you remember this connection or resource? How did it make you feel emotionally or physically? Show some gratitude for your capacity for connection. If you shy away from connection, bring some compassion to that protective part that wants to keep you safe.

Let's practice being present with Jesus. Let the shepherd give you rest. Whether you're grappling with hesitation or ready to trust fully. It is your place and he will refresh you. Name your dark place. Be honest with your conflict with being with Jesus. Today, I am especially thinking about_____.

Receive his rest. Allow him to lead you beside the quiet waters. God's hands are gentle, His ways soft. He will guide you, step by step, knowing which bramble to unwind your weary soul from first, then the next, and the next. Allow yourself the time to go through this cleansing process.

Ask others to allow you the time as well. None of us can measure our time detangling with anyone else's. It may take a few months, or a couple of years. If we rest in His all-knowing timeframe, we experience our safe place, which transcends time and space. He wants to be our dwelling place.

He will redeem you and restore you to the safety of the flock where soft grass caresses you and refreshing waters bubble.

Whenever you feel the bramble tighten again, stop, find a quiet place, and breathe. Allow His balm to ooze into your soul. Break the bonds of shame and accept His merciful grace. You are no longer lost.

Our Lord uses many ways to free us from the mess in our lives. Be open to them and let Him do His job. Mentors, accountability friends, and counselors can help be Jesus' hands in your unwrapping. So can Pastors and other leaders in our lives who will walk alongside of you in this journey. People who support your healing.

At RECOVER Me, we seek to help you through this time of entanglement, little sheep. Your Father loves you and wants you to graze in green pastures by still waters to restore your soul. (Psalm 23). You can create your safe place in God by allowing Him to provide the means He knows will eventually manifest healing to you.

Prayer Matters

Let's relax in the loving arms of our Redeemer. Feel free to add to this prayer or modify it as you are led. I am grateful for_____. Lord, thank You for seeking me out. I know I have been lost, stuck in the branches of_____ that have caused me pain. The more I struggle to free myself, the more entangled I become. My unhealthy attachments are strangling me.

Help me to be free from this mess. Lead me out of the dark wood and back into Your light where I can find safe rest in You, now, in this life as well as in the life to come. Let the work You are doing in me be a witness for others who are also lost and entangled.

In Jesus, name, I pray. Amen.

Notes

Chapter 4 Open Your Heart to New Ways of Being

Words of Life

"How will this be," Mary asked the angel, "since I am a virgin?"

The angel answered, "The Holy Spirit will come on you, and the power of the Most High will overshadow you. So the holy one to be born will be called[b] the Son of God. Even Elizabeth, your relative is going to have a child in her old age, and she who was said to be unable to conceive is in her sixth month. For no word from God will ever fail."

"I am the Lord's servant," Mary answered. "May your word to me be fulfilled." Then the angel left her.

At that time Mary got ready and hurried to a town in the hill country of Judea, where she entered Zechariah's home and greeted Elizabeth. When Elizabeth heard Mary's greeting, the baby leaped in her womb, and Elizabeth was filled with the Holy Spirit.   Luke 1:34-41

Attachment Matters

It might seem strange that I, a barren woman who has struggled with that stigma, would choose these verses of two miraculous pregnancies. I agree. And to be honest, for a long time I was both drawn to and repelled by these verses. I had hope that perhaps God would shine this pleasure on me, and then experienced deep disappointment because He hadn't. Or wouldn't.

But there is so much more richness in this story. And once I began to detach from my dark wood, I was able to see it, like a lighted path leading back into the sunshine-lit fields. There are two deep truths I see. Let me share that with you.

First Truth

There is a misconception, especially among Western cultures, that we are all to be loners. Pull up our bootstraps, put on our big-girl panties, and "just do it." If anything needs to be done, it is up to us. No one else. In this land of opportunity, it's hustle bustle and grind hard. Survival of the fittest — or the most cunning, or the most influential.

The Bible is not a book about "Jesus and Me." Yes, He is our Savior and we each must make the same decision Mary did, that is to let Him come into our lives, our hearts, and yes, our own physical bodies. 1 John 3:24 states that, *"The one who keeps God's commands lives in him, and he in them. And this is how we know that he lives in us: We know it by the Spirit he gave us."* But notice the verse doesn't say "dwell in *you*" or "gave *you*." It talks in the plural. Us.

The ancient Hebrews believed in a communal God. He dwelt amongst them. They were His people. Today it is the same. We are a Body of Christ, and as Paul states in 1 Corinthians 12:37, *Now you are the body of Christ, and each one of you is a part of it.* We need each other to function.

I think that is why the Holy Spirit told Mary of her cousin Elizabeth, and why Mary went to visit her. Sure, Mary needed to "get out of Dodge" for fear of being stoned when she began to show that she had a child in her womb and had not yet been taken to Joseph's matrimony bed. But more than that, she needed that woman-to-woman companionship. Don't you think the elderly Elizabeth had faced a few raised eyebrows as well?

Women need each other. In past generations, our ancestors quilted together, harvested together, cooked together, and raised their children together. Multigenerational living was the norm. It is not so today. So, women try to connect on social media or in groups that share hobbies. Or perhaps they seek out the Church, the Body where hopefully women can be themselves—with all their doubts, fears, strength, and joys —and minister to each other as they face different trials and stages of life.

Mary needed Elizabeth and vice versa. The saying that there is strength in numbers is very true. We need each other to bolster us, and to keep each of us accountable. But the attachments must be in Christ, so they remain healthy and free of human sins such as jealousies or favoritism. Only then can there be an atmosphere where we can dare to be open and vulnerable — not to bleed all over everyone else all the time, but to ask for help in binding our wounds through prayer, wise guidance from those who have been there, and by studying the Word.

As I stated in Chapter Two, I was raised in a family of strong women, but they were stoic ladies, too. None of them taught me the proper way to lean on each other, or counsel each other, or reveal our wounds so they can have the ointment of fellowship applied to them. We didn't pray over each other. Instead, we prayed for each other in our respective places. So, when I was in pain and lost in the brambles of disappointment, I didn't have the free ticket to go to any of them. My "Americanism" kicked in. Do it by myself. Suffer in silence. I desperately needed an Elizabeth in my life. But there were none, or so I thought. Maybe there was one for me. I would not have known because my perpetual shame caused me to hide that wounded part of me.

One woman who came to RECOVER Me was from an African culture where feelings are not shared openly with others. Highly educated in an analytical field, such ideas were foreign to her, and a bit scary. However, after several miscarriages, which she had not allowed herself to process through, she found herself overwhelmed with fear for the children she had carried to term and delivered. Yet she was hesitant to love them fully in case something happened to them and she experienced the anguish all over again. She writes:

"I was invited to attend one session of the "recover me" class as an observer. I became a participant and found healing. It has given me more of an insight into understanding me, the world and God. It first starts off learning about love of God, sharing experiences, finding that safe place in God but then when you get neat to the middle of the sessions, something drops. It gets very personal and makes you reflect. Before I knew it, my deepest pain and emotions were laid out like a roadmap. This book gave me the guidance, courage, and hope to acknowledge and reconcile with God, myself, and others.

Don't hesitate. If you want to walk in freedom. Share the book with others and register for the next session. – PM"

I encourage each of you to seek out your Mary to whom you can minister but also your Elizabeth to whom you can not only pray with but receive guidance from when you need it. Dwight Lynn Moody, the founder of the Moody Bible Institute in the late 1800's has been known to have said that the engine of the church, i.e. the thing that kept it going, was praying women.

We need each other to thrive. Otherwise, we only survive.

Second Truth

Mary was bold enough and had faith enough to change her course. *"I am the Lord's servant... May your word to me be fulfilled."*

I had my agenda, my heart's desire. Scripture said God would give me my heart's desire. Why hadn't He?

I had ignored the first part of that verse of Psalm 37:4 – *to take delight in the Lord*. To bend my will to His. To realize He ordered the universe and knows the future. I don't. I had been treating Him like a Celestial Santa Claus. Hadn't I been good? Hadn't I accepted Christ as my Savior and tried to confess my sins? Well, then...?

Mary's humbled obedience has taught me to quit fighting the brambles as discussed in the last chapter. Trust more in God's will unfolding in my life. Let Him work at releasing me from any unhealthy attachments so I can be attached to the right ones He leads me to find.

Joseph was the right man for Mary. God knew that. Joseph honored her and believed her. He cared for her and raised her son, God's Son. Because Mary had attached herself to God, He attached her to Joseph. And when she was widowed, her son, Jesus, cared for her. On the cross, He gave her to his best friend, John so he would take care of her as if she were his own mother, as was the tradition of the time.

Mary's spent her life bending to God's will for her, ready to change directions or behavior as He willed. She opened her heart to new challenges with trust and faith. She walked in the Light, and never ventured into the dark wood even when her life had darkened moments.

Water for the Soul

When Elizabeth's child, John, leapt in her womb and she told Mary she was the most blessed among women, that was the affirmation Mary needed. She broke out in a prayerful song, which is recorded in Luke, Chapter I and is known as "The Magnificat".

And Mary said:

"My soul glorifies the Lord
47 and my spirit rejoices in God my Savior,
48 for he has been mindful
  of the humble state of his servant.
From now on all generations will call me blessed,
49 for the Mighty One has done great things for me—
  holy is his name.
50 His mercy extends to those who fear him,
  from generation to generation.
51 He has performed mighty deeds with his arm;
  he has scattered those who are proud in their inmost thoughts.
52 He has brought down rulers from their thrones
  but has lifted up the humble.
53 He has filled the hungry with good things
  but has sent the rich away empty.
54 He has helped his servant Israel,
  remembering to be merciful
55 to Abraham and his descendants forever,
  just as he promised our ancestors."

Instead of worrying about her life, her reputation, or her future, she put her trust solely in God. She acknowledged that He is Mighty and cares for us. He had done great things, though many would see being pregnant before your wedding night as not so great. She didn't ask why? She had asked how (Luke 1:34), and that was okay.

We can ask God to show us, but it is His decision whether it is best for us to know. Sometimes, we only need to see the next step in front of us in the fog and trust that He will clear the path ahead or provide us the means to walk it. Just as He did with Mary, each step of the way in her life.

Was it free of sorrow? No. She had to pack up, leave her homeland and people, and head to a foreign country to save her and her baby's life. She was widowed at a young age. She watched her son die on a cross. But she was correct. Generations would call her blessed. Why? She opened her heart to God's ways and changed her desires to meet His.

She knew His mercy would extend to those who feared (revered) Him. She recalled His mighty deeds and that gave her the confidence that He could do them again and again. He was a God who kept His promises. He ruled the universe. She could trust in Him and attach herself to Him. She knew He would be mindful of her and protect her.

We can as well. Let's get some practical skills.

Way of the Redeemed

Anger is a common reaction to loss. It often used to ward off the more difficult feelings of shame, guilt, or emptiness. Historically, women have been subjected to the unfavorable criticism regarding their feelings of anger even if these feelings were appropriate. Generally, it has caused us to suppress our anger, which studies suggest that can lead to higher rates of certain types of cancer, high blood pressure, and cardiovascular disease.

Men are often far more physically aggressive. Women are more likely to turn their anger from losses, such as relationships, time, or dreams inwardly. One expression of this is to deny our own wants and needs in unhealthy ways. When was the last time that you made yourself a real priority?

Listed below are some skills and strategies to ensure that you honor yourself.

Saying "Yes" to Yourself

This begins with developing your ability to say "No" to other people or lesser priorities. This is critical to self-compassion. You may feel awkward about being assertive because the people in your life may have grown accustomed to your constantly neglecting your own needs. They may get upset, or they may support your self-compassion, but take one step at a time to reach this essential goal of recovering yourself.

Here are a few reflection considerations or questions to saying "Yes" to yourself when you have been presented with a request from another person.

Take some time to consider the request. Ask for a few hours or a few days to pray and evaluate the request. Responding quickly to the pressure in the moment often leads to regret and you being angry at yourself.

Do I have the emotional or physical capacity to handle this person's needs? Oftentimes we feel pressured to take it on and put off doing things for ourselves.

Is fear causing me to lean toward saying "Yes" to this person's request? Am I sending the wrong message about the person's worth or my self-worth by constantly fulfilling their needs?

What resources do I need to fulfill my God-given dreams? Is God providing opportunities, but you are too busy and stressed to recognize them?

Am I procrastinating in a specific area of my life? Will fulfilling this need continue this toxic cycle in my life?

What can I comfortably give? Ask for clarification of all that is being asked. Suggest that you only do a part of what is being asked or actually saying, "No."

Reflect on what it would be like to communicate your response to others. What can you do to tolerate the distress of disappointing others?

Consider New Ways of Caring for Your Body

Upon assessing my entire health history and current functioning, one of my medical professionals told me that I was moving from surviving and striving to the place of thriving. It was strange to hear this language from a medical practitioner. These words **Survive, Strive, and Thrive** strengthened my resolve to recover my own health and healing.

I began to show grace and compassion toward that unresolved part of me — that little girl who used food to cope with any anxious thoughts. I thanked her for her care, but I set her free as I have learned new ways to care for my body. My RECOVER Me process has been of one of discovery.

Below are listed several interventions that are beneficial for the body. The beauty is that they also benefit the soul and invigorate the spirit as well.

Deep Tissue Massage Therapy is used to relieve muscle tension through direct pressure being applied to the surface of the muscles. This revitalizing experience identifies stiff or sore areas, and slowly works to loosen the layers of muscle tissue. Various hand positions and movement are then used to respond to different tissue qualities.

Therapeutic Stretching is used to reduce tension and may decrease the intensity of joint discomfort. Stretching right after a massage enhances the benefits of massage therapy. Ask a massage therapist about how to properly use this technique.

Reflexology is a skilled treatment of your feet involving both pressure points and massage. This therapy deals with the principle that there are reflexes in the feet that directly correspond to each organ and every part of the body. This has become very popular because of its minimal side effects and because it is pain free. The benefits of Reflexology are the release of toxins and increased energy.

Biofeedback therapy or training supports your body's ability to relieve stress naturally. Personally, it has been helpful in improving my own sleep quality and reducing my overall anxiety. The feedback that you receive through various methods that may include heart rate, brain wave, breathing, or muscle contractions. These inform you of new ways to improve your health condition or enhance your physical performance. It is noted to help with conditions such as, Attention Deficit Hyperactive Disorder, Irritable Bowel Syndrome, migraines, and insomnia. You can receive biofeedback therapy in medical centers, hospitals, private practice, or physical therapy clinics. Please make sure that you choose a trained biofeedback therapist. Like most medical professionals, the trained biofeedback therapist performs tests to gather information by utilizing specialized equipment. A biofeedback machine converts physiological signals, such as brain waves or heat rates, into meaningful information. Biofeedback machines that can be used to perform these tests include MRI brain scans and skin surface scans. Beware of biofeedback devices being marketed for home use.

Exercise Intervention means regular exercise, which promotes positive brain health. It can generate new cells while maintaining existing cells. It also promotes cognition including one's ability to remember information, pay attention, and to think quickly. It is important to rediscover exercise as an important intervention for healing and protecting both the body and the mind. Some exercises to consider include dancing, cycling, running, gardening, and swimming. Walking and stretching can be good first steps to a more active exercise habit. If you are new to the group exercises or are not ready for the gym, stretching can be a gentle way to ease your way into the workout regimen.

Progressive Muscle Relaxation is an intervention that is free, and you can administer to yourself. It can relieve stress and tension from the body.

Find a quiet place free from distractions. Sit in a comfortable chair or lay comfortably on a mat or a bed.

We will do each muscle group from head to feet.
Take three deep breaths.
As you breathe in, tense your right hand and forearm
Relax your right hand and forearm
As you breathe in, tense your right upper arm
Relax your right upper arm
As you breathe in, tense your left hand and forearm
Relax your left hand and forearm
As you breathe in, tense your left upper arm
Relax your left upper arm
As you breathe in, tense your forehead
Relax your forehead
As you breathe in, tense your eyes and cheeks
Relax your eyes and cheeks

As you breathe in, tense your mouth and jaw
Relax your mouth and jaw
As you breathe in, tense your neck
Relax your neck
As you breathe in, tense your shoulders
Relax your shoulders
As you breathe in, tense your shoulder blades and back
Relax your shoulder blades and back
As you breathe in, tense your chest and stomach
Relax your chest and stomach
As you breath in, tense your hips and buttocks
Relax your hips and buttocks
As you breathe in, tense your right upper leg
Relax your right upper leg
As you breathe in, tense your right lower leg
Relax your right lower leg
As you breathe in, tense your right foot
Relax your right foot
As you breathe in, tense your left upper leg
Relax your left upper leg
As you breathe in, tense your left lower leg
Relax your left lower leg
As you breathe int tense your left foot
Relax your left foot

Enjoy this relaxed state for a while and return to your daily routine.

Identify a Mentor to serve as a guide as you move through your personal dark wood

Being open to mentoring can lead you through dark wood with purpose. Mentors can speak wisdom into your life during confusing times. But how do we know that we are getting a mentor that is a good fit?

First, let's look at types of mentoring relationships. There are more formalized mentoring relationships assigned through, professional work settings, churches, and other groups. I am a part of the SHINE Mentorship which pairs trained mentors to mentee for approximately a year period.

There are informal mentoring pairings that develop over time. These close friendships have stood the test of time and the natural progression is mutual trust.

There are also consultant type mentors in which you glean a great deal of knowledge usually from specialized information from the mentor.

Commit to praying for the type of mentor that you should pursue. It may be someone that is in your life. The person may be older or maybe not your first choice. Reflect on a goal that you have. It may be an emotional, physical, or creative goal.

Once this person is identified. Reach out and make your request know to her.

Welcoming Rest

When you feel a bit lost in the dark wood and the thorns of trees begin to scratch, recall Mary's song. Read it and let it seep into your heart. Open your mind, soul and spirit to God and seek His ways. Allow Him to minister to you, be it through other fellowshipping with godly women, Scripture, hymns, or counseling. Or all of the above.

Be open to have your heart pulled in a different direction and take on the behavior of humility and trust. It is not easy, but the results are worth the effort, and God will send His Spirit to assist you.

Find a quiet place, even if it is the bathroom or the front seat of your car. Close your eyes. Breathe out your stress and breathe in God's presence. Recall the times He has come through for you, and if you can't ask Him to bring it to mind. He won't mind. Psalm 111:4 says, *"He has caused his wonders to be remembered; the Lord is gracious and compassionate."*

Whisper, or shout it out:

"My soul magnifies the Lord and my spirit rejoices in God my Savior, for her has been mindful of the humble state of his servant...me."

Say it over and over until your mind begins to align with your heart. Then be still and listen for God's response. It may not come immediately but have faith. He will begin to untangle you and set you back on the right path as the Good Shepherd does. One step at a time.

Prayer Matters

Lord, my soul does magnify You. I give back to you my losses perceived or actual. I may not know what You have planned, but I bend my will to You, and I give You my heart, mind, and soul. Especially about this _____ that is so heavy on my mind.

Help me to seek out the Mary or Elizabeth in my life to journey with me. Give me the humility to trust you and the boldness to find my strength in You and the mentor that you have assigned to me. I cannot do this on my own. I need You and others that you have assigned to my life. I will pay it forward by helping other women nurture what you have birthed in her. Forgive me for comparing myself to others for I am uniquely gifted. I ask you to show me how to make space for new births in my life.

I trust in You, Lord. Amen.

Notes:

Chapter 5 Voice Your Boundaries

Words of Life

The one who enters by the gate is the shepherd of the sheep. The gatekeeper opens the gate for him, and the sheep listens to his voice. He calls his own sheep by name and leads them out. When he has brought out all his own, he goes on ahead of them, and his sheep follow him because they know his voice. But they will never follow a stranger; in fact, they will run away from him because they do not recognize a stranger's voice." … "I am the good shepherd. The good shepherd lays down his life for the sheep… "My sheep listen to my voice; I know them, and they follow me."
John 10:3-5,11,27

Attachment Matters

As humans we tend to blur boundaries. We follow our hearts and go where angels fear to tread, sometimes for the sakes of our loved ones, our kids, our family. Black and white turn to shades of grayness.

There are other boundaries that we blur, all for the sake of being accepted. To avoid conflict and ensure love, we allow people to overstep the bounds. We let them walk all over us as if we are door mats. We think it is the loving thing to do, but it isn't because we do not hold anyone accountable. And if they are not accountable for their actions, they will never change.

What voices are you listening to? The ones of rejection? The demeaning ones that say you will never be pretty enough, good enough or smart enough. The one that says don't talk back. Don't stand up for yourself. Don't cause conflict or he/she/they may reject you.

As women, we are all way too familiar with the societal standard of remaining quiet. IF we deviate and dare to express ourselves, we are seen as difficult.

We've all heard them, and more often than we want to admit, have not only listened to them but followed them instead of the voice of our loving Lord. We let people steal our joy, our sense of worth, and our lives. Instead of running away from these negative influences, we follow the stranger deeper into the dark wood. We turn our ears to the howling wolves instead of tuning in to the still quiet voice of the Holy Spirit. We trade the positive, inspiring, uplifting messages of love and comfort our Lord provides and instead grab onto the negative ones of other humans that reinforce our low self-esteem.

It is better to shut up and try to shut out the hurt than to chance rejection. Don't rock the boat. Don't ruffle feathers. Stay below the radar. In doing so, the natural boundaries around our hearts and our minds slowly crumble, leaving us vulnerable and not knowing what will happen next.

It is what psychologists call codependency and some of us women have mastered it. The abuser, whether emotional or physical, depends on us to be their battering ram. We depend on them for the love they offer and to provide, hoping this is just a phase, and peace will once again reign...for a while.

We trade self-esteem for companionship because none of us want to be alone. Our hearts and minds are not wired that way. Loneliness is what we secretly fear the most, in spite of the fact we'd all love a bit more "me" time now and then.

Some of us chuck it all in and set off on our own "Thelma and Louise adventure." Enough of the codependent life. We want to live. Do our own thing. We kick over our boundaries and head out, free, and wild. But soon we get lost. We strain our ears to hear the familiar voices, even the negative ones. For example, if we had abusive fathers, we tend to hook up with or marry abusive partners or even work for them.

Sometimes, brambles and dark wood are comfortable because they are way too familiar. *We all, like sheep, have **gone astray**, each of us has turned to our own way* (Isaiah 53:6).

We have traded one destructive behavior for another. One wolf for a bear.

Water for the Soul

In the ancient world, shepherds herded sheep in free-grazing fields and meadows. There were no fences. No private property. It was not uncommon for several herds to all intermingle. But each sheep knew its shepherd's call and followed him because they knew he'd protect them from predators that hungrily roamed the hills. If a sheep strayed, especially a young vulnerable one, the shepherd would leave the flock to be watched by another shepherd and go find the animal. Sheep often get so busy grazing that they don't look up to see where they are going. They get caught in brambles, or tumble over a shallow cliff.

In Psalm 23, David says that God's rod and staff comfort him. The rod was like a Billy club the policemen used in the 1800's. It was made of wood or a rock stitched inside of a tough leather sleeve, like a small baseball bat. The shepherd would literally whack away the wolves with it. The staff was a long pole with a hook on it that the shepherd would use to upright a sheep if it tumbled over on its back, or to grab it by the body and lift it out of weeds or back up a cliff. Both were of comfort because they were life savers. David is saying basically that God is his protector. When the Creator of the Universe watches your back, that is a pretty comforting thought, right?

Shepherds would lead their flocks to a common paddock in the evenings. These were large enclosed meadows with embankments of dirt and rocks surrounding them and a small opening in front from which the sheep could enter. The shepherds would then lay out their sleeping rolls and become the "gate" to keep the sheep in and the predators and thieves, creeping in the night from the dark woods, out.

In the morning as the sun rose to light the world, each shepherd would sound out his call and his sheep would wake up and follow him back to the green pastures and still waters.

Do you see the connection to what Jesus says in John, Chapter 10? As long as we are in the range of His voice, we are in safe boundaries. Night and day. Even in the dark wood of our lives, we can still hear Him calling us out.

Yes, life may distract us. We keep our heads down just trying to make it through one more day. We focus on the problem, the loneliness, the hurt, the anger instead of on our Savior. We are now vulnerable to attacks —verbal, emotional, and perhaps physical.

We take our eyes off the Shepherd and that almost always ends up badly. We can trip and fall into danger or get caught up in the brambles of sin's temptations. The snarls of those who may wish to harm us fill our ears.

That is when we cry out for help. The Shepherd hears our pleas and comes to comfort us with the rod or the staff. It may come as a hug to His chest, or as a discipline to lead us back on the right path. But the Shepherd always has our best interest at heart.

Do we trust His voice? Do we wander freely in the boundaries Scripture sets for us, or are we tempted to head for what appears to be greener pastures? Perhaps it is a handsome man who lures us in with sweet talk, a more prestigious job which may mean distorting our ethics, or a fun, but a tad bit wild, friend that tempts us to stay for one more drink instead of heading home. Don't ignore the gatekeeper (Holy Spirit's warnings) and let them into our lives.

It takes guts to voice your opinion. To say that you are not letting the old patterns rule you, that you will set secure boundaries around yourself. No longer the doormat for everyone to use and will no longer be the target of abuse. You take the chance of losing their love, and instead follow the One who loves unconditionally, whose peace is beyond understanding will guard your heart and mind. (Philippians 4:7).

Whose voice will you follow? Will you let Him lead you into safe boundaries where you can feel secure, comfort and protection? No one says you have to do this alone.

At RECOVER Me, we teach you how to set and live within these safe, strong boundaries.

Just as the ancient world shepherd built up rocks and earth to create a boundary for his sheep from things that lurk in darkness, our Lord will help you build good boundaries so you can thrive in lush, green pastures.

Once you tune into His voice and follow it, you will find your voice, and it will be loving, but strong, firm, and protective...just like His.

Isn't that what we really wanted in our relationships in the first place?

Way of the Redeemed

There are steps we can take to follow the Shepherd's voice out of our dark wood into the lush, green pastures by still waters.

1. *Write down* what you desire most. For example, comfort, love, security, companionship?

2. *Use and online or book Concordance* of Scripture verses to look up passages in the Bible that show how God can be those things. In truth, He is the only One who can be all the time, without fail. Why? Because God is good. That is His nature. He is not tainted by selfish, human nature.

3. *Memorize* them as arsenal, your rod and staff. Sticky-note post them to your fridge, mirror, your computer monitor, or the visor of your car. Tape them inside your desk drawer, carry them in your wallet. Secure them in your journal or in the notes section of your smartphone. Place them around your life like boundaries. Even when you don't see them anymore, your brain will. More and more the positive, loving Word will secure you.

4. *Pray*. An adage states that a day knotted by prayer in the morning and at night will not unravel. Stop and pray during the day while stuck at a traffic light or in line at the bank or grocery store. Pray when negative feelings begin to bubble up. Pray when people want to shove you back into the codependent lifestyle you had.

5. *Then take time to listen* for the Voice. The more you "hear it" in your heart, the more you will recognize it and heed it.

6. *Make Jesus the first man* in your life, and all of your other relationships will eventually fall into a healthy place with strong boundaries. Let your Shepherd love and accept you and let Him show you how to see your worth through His eyes of grace.

Welcoming Rest

Take two deep breaths as you exhale naturally

What do you notice about your body? Do you feel tightness in your chest or shoulder? Is there a dull ache in your head or belly?

Take two grounding breaths and exhale.

Notice your thoughts, do not judge them, but pay attention to the theme. The rate in which they come and go.

Take as many breaths that you need to gently interrupt getting lost in your thoughts.

Pay attention to your feelings. They directly impact the way that you feel. Again, no judgment, just notice the fleeting nature of your feelings.

Take some deep and grounding breaths.

What do you need at this moment?

Settle your mind and heart and listen.

Maybe your body needs to move?

Or have a hug or a nap?

Maybe your mind needs a break or to take delight in a book that you have not read yet or a movie to watch with new eyes?

Maybe your heart needs to tell someone where you are right now?

Or to abstain from talk.

Maybe your spirit needs to settle as the Lord does the work of re-establishing you. Or simply just be.

Prayer Matters

Lord, thank you that You are our Shepherd. You care for us, love us unconditionally and only want the best for us. You send Your Holy Spirit to secure our boundaries and keep us from harm. Because we feel secure in Your love and comfort, we can be bold enough to voice our boundaries and warn You when we feel the predators of our past negative actions and reactions lurking nearby. Thank you for always guiding us, protecting us, and loving us just as we are, your sheep. Amen.

Notes

Chapter 6   Explore your Purpose

Words of Life

My soul follows close behind You; Your right hand upholds me.   Psalm 63:8

Attachment Matters

Dante Alighieri, who wrote the famous poem, *The Divine Comedy* in 1308, knew what it was like to get caught in a dark place. The harshness of the dark wood may result in fear. Fear can grip the heart as we move through the hard part of our journey. As humans, we have a natural inclination to avoid actions or under-function, in order to escape the pain of disappointment. We may rely too heavily on the opinions of others regarding our life experiences. It seems easier to value the image of control more than to value the One can give it to us.

The truth is that most people are too absorbed in their own problems to really notice our situation. Many times, the people with unhealthy attachments stand to benefit the most from our failure to move forward from our lost places. It is healthy to grieve the loss of a loved one or a dream. It is not healthy to zone out from our lives.

Other times, we unknowingly over-function to try to heal the trauma or grief from the losses that we have experienced on our way. We do this by doing for others the things they can do for themselves. Do you give advice and get upset when others don't appreciate it? Do you perceive it as rejection of yourself as a person? We distract ourselves by becoming "over-functioners" appearing that we are cool, calm, and collected. I've heard many women say," I don't look like what I have been through." I get the positive and overcoming sentiment, but some of us need to worry less about what we look like and place more value on whatever we are attached to that is causing us to stall on our journeys.

This was me, over-functioning and focusing on the needs of others. I was overwhelmed and did not pay attention to my body's cry for rest until a stroke in the latter part of 2016 forced me to reevaluate my coping methods.

The frightening part of this brain injury was that it took place at night. For starters, I was not getting proper rest. I was sleeping throughout the night without getting a good, quality rest.

I had an undiagnosed sleep disorder. The morning of the stroke was like most morning routines—morning prayer and reading of the Word, breakfast, and small talk with my husband. Gwynmar remembers me singing and dancing as I prepared for work that morning.

As soon as I reached my workplace—and yes, I drove over 30 minutes to my destination—my speech began to slur. I went to my colleague's office and began to cry as I felt the numbness encompass my right side. I could not write, and I had much difficulty lifting my right foot.

I felt disconnected more than ever from my body, but strangely compassionate for all it had gone through up until this point. The failed In-vitro Inseminations and various medical interventions had taken its toll on me. I was frightened by my vulnerability, but a keen awareness of God's love for me now enveloped me on all sides.

From this point on through my physical recovery, I began to embark on this RECOVER Me of reconnection.

I say this with all self-compassion, many factors may have contributed to the stroke that I had experienced, but as I look back over my life, I can recall those times that the Redeemer was offering me a gentler way. I began to follow the Redeemer more closely. He led me to practical ways that brought healing and redemption of purpose to my body, soul, and spirit.

Let's explore a passionate woman who also followed the Redeemer! Her resolve during desperate times has inspired me to let go of the shame in my own life and pursue my purpose.

Water for the Soul

Even if you are somewhat unfamiliar with the Bible on some level, you are most likely aware of the women Eve, Esther, and Mary. However, I think it is important to acknowledge the many unnamed women in the Bible.

This is a challenge to discover or go deeper into the contributions of these unnamed women. Women could not legally be counted in a census or even be educated. Many women were confined and could not preach, especially when men were present during the early fellowship of the church. Even during these times, there is a real temptation to treat their stories as insignificant.

One woman, though never named, is significant enough to be mentioned in three of the Gospels. This woman's story is found in Matthew 9, Mark 5 and Luke 8. She is known as the woman with the issue of blood. She had suffered from a menstrual period continually for 12 long years.

This woman was very isolated. No one would have wanted to be around her since she could not go out in public.

In our recent world, we have grown familiar with quarantine practices due to the outbreak of the Coronavirus 19.

During 2020, many of us were quarantined with our family, or a familiar group of friends, or totally isolated and alone. Our typical coping skills of going to work, the gym, and spending time with friends were shut down. We are still learning the negative effects on mental health that the COVID-19 pandemic has taken on us.

However, this woman spent an exceptionally long time quarantined from all people including her family. Why was that? She had been considered regularly unclean due to her non-stop bleeding condition according to Jewish law (see Leviticus 15). This problem affected every area of her life.

The Bible records in Luke Chapter 8 that she spent all her money on physicians trying to get well. My mind immediately imagines her exhaustion from trying to manage the social logistics of it all. I also wonder the level of difficulty that she must have faced earning a steady source of income. Moreover, I wonder if she had been single or had been divorced since she could not conceive due to her condition.

Let's take a look at the text in Mark 5:24-34.

> *So Jesus went with him. A large crowd followed and pressed around him. And a woman was there who had been subject to bleeding for twelve years. She had suffered a great deal under the care of many doctors and had spent all she had, yet instead of getting better she grew worse. When she heard about Jesus, she came up behind him in the crowd and touched his cloak, because she thought, "If I just touch his clothes, I will be healed." Immediately her bleeding stopped, and she felt in her body that she was freed from her suffering.*
>
> *At once Jesus realized that power had gone out from him. He turned around in the crowd and asked, "Who touched my clothes?"*
>
> *"You see the people crowding against you," his disciples answered, "and yet you can ask, 'Who touched me?'"*
>
> *But Jesus kept looking around to see who had done it. Then the woman, knowing what had happened to her, came and fell at his feet and, trembling with fear, told him the whole truth. He said to her, "Daughter, your faith has healed you. Go in peace and be freed from your suffering."*

I loved the way that she imagined Jesus healing her before she pursued him. Despite her struggles and ascribed "uncleanness" she was desperate, yet determined, to follow Jesus. This woman did not let her marginalized position in society stop her. She pressed into the crowd to reach Jesus. The Redeemer responded by inquiring about the person who touched Him. Though the crowds pressed against Him, it was her touch that registered due to her determination and faith.

Her last hope was Jesus, and he healed her body. She was no longer the woman with the bleeding issue. Her faith had activated that redemption.

Way of the Redeemed

I can relate to her story after the turmoil associated with my body not functioning properly. With years of infertility, and the brain injury that I experienced, I did not notice that my body was grieving, too. But it was. It had been through years of IVF, surgery, and other assisted reproductive interventions.

I needed to deal with my own loss of a child directly, but gently. I knew about stress management because I had been a mental health therapist for over 20 years, but I knew I had to go deeper. I went through the healing to process of my body, soul, and spirit.

What about you? Are you ready to press through the crowd to reach out to Jesus and have Him heal you?

Here are some practical ways to pursue deeper healing.

1. Identify and journal the areas of unfulfilled expectations that you still hold anger. This anger can be toward yourself, persons who betrayed you, or even God. Anger is usually the second emotion. Secondly, write down the first emotions that may have proceeded the anger. For example, rejection and disappointment.

2. Write a letter to release the person, the place, or the season that you experienced the anger, hurt, fear, rejection, or disappointment.

Here is my grief letter that I wrote to my daughter that never came.

My Sweet Girl,

I am writing this letter to say goodbye to you. I know that you never came in the flesh, but the way I hoped for you, well, let's say, you were very real to me. You were more than a dream. You were everything to me. Gwynmar and I named you Zoe Sanaa. You would have loved him. He is already a great dad. He always wanted to see me with a daughter.

My husband also enjoyed watching me interact with his mother, Celeste, and my mom, Rose, who are super close to my heart. You would have loved them too. Gwynmar helped me come up with your name. Zoe has the Greek meanings of alive and life. Sanaa has Swahili and Arabic meanings of shining light and a work of art. He knew of the fears I had about giving birth to a son. My younger brother, Henry, was pulled over not far from our family home. It was a scary situation. Thank God my mom was driving by and saw these plain clothes officers searching his car. These police officers assured my mother that they were just doing "routine and regular checks" with no other drivers being stopped for these checks. The situation left me perplexed and cautious.

You would have loved your Uncle Henry. He is funny and he has a son, Jaylen, too. He graduated with a degree in engineering so that makes him incredibly and annoyingly detailed. My life has been blessed with adult children, two sons in laws, and energetic grandkids that I simply adore.

So, I hoped, I believed, and I even tried many medical procedures to assist in your arrival. I watched others give birth to their babies. Some of them had various problems trying to conceive, and yet I prayed for them. It was hard at times to celebrate with them. It was a bitter reminder that I was without my baby. I managed to let love shine through for them. I can't be a hater. I genuinely loved seeing the life that God creates. God is good when you yield your hurt to Him, but I just wanted Him to give you to me.

After trying many medical interventions from IUI to IVF to assist in your arrival, I was discouraged. My hope was shattered, and my body was left depleted. But my hope for you would not leave me alone. I prayed and I tried fertility diets, to no avail. For years, I wrestled in this weird part of my journey. It was an undesirable No Man's Land. Here I found myself numb but grieved. I was not free to want you because it was too painful and pitiful, but I could not let the image of you go. It was a pity party that I did not want to go to if I was honest. Shame set in, but I was living my life. Striving, attaining, church planting, and doing-all the things that we do to move on with our lives. But my body ached for you, even though my heart was afraid to desire you anymore.

I then hit a wall that literally knocked me off my feet. I had a stroke in my sleep. My neurologist said that I was a "lucky lady" to have survived such an ordeal. My right side had to be restored as well as my speech. It was hard work. I went to a great rehabilitation center Monday-Fridays from 9am-3pm. It went daily for a straight three-month period. There were no babies there, but the Redeemer found me. He was there on my walks around the lake. He was telling me all about myself—my attachments and his plans for me. I shared with the Redeemer my desires for you. I told Him your name was Zoe. He liked the name; this was my Well experience. I can see Jesus in my mind's eye smiling as I was telling Him all about you. He already knew that you were my great desire. Something began to happen as I opened myself to Jesus. The scales lifted from my eyes. He had been watching over me all this time. He was the shade on my right hand that Psalms 121 references.

As I talked to the Redeemer during my recovery, He began to remind me that I was His daughter. He told me that His plans for me are still great. He asked me to rest in Him and that peace will be multiplied in my life. He asked me to lay you down at the altar so I can live my life more abundantly. It has not been easy. I am only writing this letter because my therapist strongly suggested it.

Giving birth is a natural desire. I used to want hope to leave me alone. I wished I did not want you, Zoe. Now, I want hope to never leave me. This time I look for hope in everything that I am graced with in my life. Hope gives purpose to every part of me. Even the parts that longed for you. I know that I will think of you from time to time and even shed a tear or two for what I missed.

This was a necessary part of my journey. I am now choosing to fully engage in the next part of my life's journey. I cannot wait to see the life that he has planned for me. Bye Zoe Sanaa.

Love & Kisses,

Yolanda

Make a commitment to observe the areas in life, such as your role as a romantic partner, parent, or employee/entrepreneur. Is there a relationship in which you may be under-functioning or over-functioning? This may be good time to reach out to a trusted friend, family member, or mentor for feedback with this step. Ask Jesus to heal the parts of yourself that try to cope with the losses in life.

4. Press into the Redeemer in faith and ask for healing. He is a miracle worker that sees and feels your emptiness. I have seen Him restore health when the doctors gave a doomed prognosis. He did it for the nameless woman who had the issue of blood. Ask Jesus to heal you and any parts of your body. Be open to the ways He provides, whether it is through doctors, counselors, or a miracle. He never gave me a baby, but He healed my mind, soul, and body in so many ways.

   Ask Jesus to heal your fixed thoughts regarding the ways or methods that you should be healed. It is easy in your weariness to get stuck and to miss the purpose that the Redeemer is trying to set forth in your life.

5. Write down on a sheet of paper what you believed your purpose in life was prior to your dark wood experience. Share it with someone that you trust. Give that sheet of paper to that person. Ask that person to commit to praying for a renewed sense of purpose for you over the next three months.

6. Solidify a morning or evening routine that nurtures the body, soul, and spirit. This serves as a preventative and compassionate resting place to release your burdens and to gain instructions. Research daily self-care apps, such as the Calm app or Fabulous, which is a science-based self-care app that will help you build rituals that you design, such as meditation and gratefulness activities.

7. Seek the help of a professional if you feel mentally, physically, spiritually, or emotionally stuck. As a therapist, I find it healthy for me to seek counseling from time to time. I find that to be the epitome of self-care is recognizing that I am stuck, and I need to reach out for guidance. We all need someone skilled, such as a nutritionist, psychiatrist, or licensed mental health professional to walk alongside us. God uses many people in our journey. This saves us precious time. Pray that pride does not hinder you from embracing help. Humility and faith always lead you to His purposes for your life.

Welcoming Rest

"Continued Dependence upon You"[11]

O God my Creator and Redeemer, I may not go forth today except You accompany me with Your blessing. Let not the vigor and freshness of the morning, or the glow of good health, or the present prosperity of my undertakings, deceive me into a false reliance upon my own strength. All these good gifts have come to me from You. They were Yours to give and they are Yours to curtail. They are not mine to keep. I do but hold them in trust and only in continued dependence upon You, the Giver, can they be worthily enjoyed.

Let me then put back into Your hand all that You have given me, rededicating to Your service all the powers of my mind and body, all my worldly goods, and all my influence with others. All these, O Father, are Yours to use as You will. All these are Yours, O Christ. All these are Yours, O Holy Spirit.

Speak in my words today, think in my thoughts, and work in all my deeds. And seeing that it is Your gracious will to make use of such weak human instruments in the fulfillment of Your mighty purpose for the world. Let my life today be the channel through which some little portion of Your divine love and pity may reach the lives that are nearest to my own.

In Your solemn presence, O God, I remember all my friends and neighbors, my fellow townsfolk, and especially the poor within our gates, beseeching You that You would give me grace, so far as in me lies, to serve them in Your name. Amen.

---

[11] John Baillie, Devotional Classics, Richard J. Foster and James Bryan Smith, HarperOne, 2005

Prayer Matters

Redeemer of lost things, your Word says that you came to seek that which was lost. Today, there is so much that has changed in this world. Help me to grieve my losses so that I can have compassion on those that grieve. Heal me from unfulfilled expectations. Impart your grace and power to every person who reads this book and engages in the recovery process. Show me the way as I follow close behind You. Grant me the courage and strength to press into you. Help me see the light of renewed purpose and the joy that sustains me as I travel along the way. Amen.

Notes:

Chapter 7   Remember the Power of Hope

Words of Life

"For now, we see in a mirror indirectly, but then we will see face to face. Now I know in part, but then I will know fully, just as I have been fully known. And now these three remain: faith, hope, and love. But the greatest of these is love."

I Corinthians 13:12-13

Attachment Matters

It is easy to lose hope when a heartbreak of any kind causes you to lose your way. For me, hope was tricky. It sustained me at times. It also prolonged the loop of grief in my life. I felt that hope was making a fool out of me. I was vulnerable because I was in love with the idea of having a baby.

Can you relate? Maybe not of wanting a baby, but desiring some person, place, or thing. Did your hope for a better relationship or a future outcome lead you to keep trying over and over? It is easy to forget the power of hope through the constant failed attempts to achieve your dreams.

 I was vulnerable and I did not like it. Many of us can relate to what Brene Brown said about vulnerability in an interview with Forbes Magazine. She was raised in a "get 'er done" and "suck it up" family and culture (very Texan, German-American). "The tenacity and grit part of that upbringing has served me, but I wasn't taught how to deal with uncertainty or how to manage emotional risk." [12]

---

[12] Dan Schwabel, Forbes Magazine, April 21,2013

Leaning into that vulnerability instead of running away from the heartbreak can give you a fresh perspective on hope. Let's explore further.

In our Biblical text above, it includes hope as one of three virtues that will remain long after the superficial fades. *"And now these three remain: faith, hope, and love. But the greatest of these is love."*

We all know faith in which I lovingly refer to as "The Rockstar" of the group. It is a gift as well as a work of God. In a skeptical world, faith in God to do the impossible seems crazy. In a world that has grown tired of pandemics and polarizing politics, God has gifted us with the grace by which we can see Jesus. We can access Him, inquire of Him, and follow Him throughout the lives that we live. He is not like other failed human attachments. You can always rely on Him and that exemplifies faith.

Love is the grandest of all. Nothing that you will do or anything that has happened to you can separate you from God's unconditional love. God is the only substance in love because He is love. He loved you before the darkness set in on your journey. His love has made provision just for you. You can always lay hold of him and be assured of His love.

But why all the emphasis on hope? Sometimes, hope gets dismissed. The concept of hope has been reduced to wishful thinking or floating dreams with no weight to them. Yet, hope is the assured confidence that something that has not happened will certainly be in the future.

Hope energizes you when faith in a specific outcome fails. Hope inspires you when disappointment causes you to not believe again. Love is the most powerful virtue, but sometimes we cannot receive it. Fear and doubt settle in when love is cut off. Hope whispers, "Don't give up. Make the Redeemer your number one attachment. His love will never fail."

Water for the Soul

The apostle Paul, author of this passage, was attempting to resolve a conflict in the Corinthian church. Corinth was a major trading center having access to the Mediterranean Sea. Ships from far-away places would bring their exotic treasures to be sold there. Corinth was known for its diversity, representing people from all walks of life. Paul found this "diversity" prominent in the Corinthian church. Paul reminds the Church that these three elements, faith, hope, and love, are invaluable and necessary for the Christian's walk.

They needed to practice these three things and focus on their commonality (the gospel of Christ) rather than their differences. The message of faith, hope, and love continues to speak to us today, especially now in our "global" society.

FAITH: *"Now faith is the substance of things hoped for, the evidence of things not seen."* Hebrews 11:1

Faith is having the confidence, knowing without a doubt, God's promises are true. Though our eyes may not see them, they are there. Faith in God is overcoming, dispelling the lies that we are not worthy – PRAISE GOD we have victory!

HOPE: *"May the God of hope fill you with all joy and peace in believing, so that by the power of the Holy Spirit you may abound in hope."* Romans 15:13

"The LORD is my portion," says my soul, "therefore I will hope in him." Lamentations 3:24

The "God of hope" allows us to look forward with joyful anticipation to everything He has promised in His word. Whether it be deliverance from physical ailments or crises in our lives, God is Hope in hopeless situations. We know that He will deliver. He is not our "last" hope. He is our only hope!

LOVE: *"The steadfast love of the LORD never ceases; his mercies never come to an end; they are new every morning; great is your faithfulness."* Lamentations 3:22-23

"For God so loved the world that He gave His only begotten Son, that whoever believes in Him should not perish but have everlasting life." John 3:16

Love is having deep affection for someone or something creating passion and pleasure. How can one define the love of God that is so vast, so deep, and unending? How does one understand this unfathomable love that He would send His only Son to die for such despicable beings, enabling them to have eternal life, yet He did! Where would we be without this love? The beauty of this situation is that we don't have to understand His love, we just need to accept it.

Upon examination of the women mentioned in **Water for the Soul**—the Samaritan woman, Ruth, Naomi, and the Woman with the issue of blood -- all four were of different ethnicities, religions, and social statuses. Though diverse, all found that they all demonstrated faith, hope, and love. Having these three elements made it possible to experience their "designated intersections" with God.

With all the baggage carried by Samaritan Woman—the baggage of shame, embarrassment, and a shady past with many mistaken beliefs, God enabled her to be an overcomer. Her faith grew. She knew her only hope was found in Jesus. Not only did she develop a love for Christ, but also for the lost people of her city. She desired them to experience the same faith, hope, and love.

Naomi had suffered loss, poverty, and bitterness. She felt abandoned. She felt alone. Though Ruth had faithfully followed her, she still saw Ruth as a liability, someone she was responsible for. I'm sure she thought, "Who is responsible for me? Who will take care of me?"

As the relationship between her and her daughter-in-law evolved, God enabled her to see and experience His faithfulness, giving her hope for each day. She found God's love to be constant and sure.

Ruth also experienced loss and poverty, but unbeknownst to Naomi, she saw something in Naomi's life that she wanted. She wanted Naomi's God. Having been born and raised in Moab, she knew of the pagan gods and wanted no part of them. Hers is a story of how her child-like faith, optimism, and love blossomed into a new life with Jehovah God elevating her, allowing her to be included in the genealogy of Christ.

When we first meet the Woman with the issue of blood, she is isolated, frustrated, and sick with only a glimmer of hope left within. We can only imagine the depth of her despair. What we can see is that that glimmer of hope igniting as she heard Jesus was coming. With increasing faith, she presses through the crowd to touch the hem of his garment. Her faith was rewarded with the healing of her body. She can now step out of the darkness into the light of His love. Jesus declared that her faith made her whole.

My prayer for you is that you practice, faith, hope, and love. That your faith increases daily, and as this happens, not only will you have hope in the Lord, but establish in your heart, He is your only hope. *"Love God with all your heart, soul, mind and strength"* (Matthew 22:37) while knowing He loves you unconditionally, lavishly, and forever.

It sounds too nice, right? Okay, let's get practical application in the next section.

Way of The Redeemed

Harriet Tubman is one of the most inspiring figures in all American history. She said," she would listen carefully to the voice of God as she led slaves north, and she would only go where she felt God led her. Fellow abolitionist Thomas Garrett said of her, "I never met any person of any color who had more confidence in the voice." [13]Harriet was an African American woman born into slavery, but God lead her all the way to freedom.

Life was hard, but she did not get stuck. Harriet suffered many weaknesses—abuses by an overseer and a chronic illness as a result of his abuse.

---

[13] .Lewis, Jone Johnson. "Biography of Harriet Tubman: Freed Slaves, Fought for the Union Army." ThoughtCo, Feb. 11, 2020, thoughtco.com/harriet-tubman-biography-3529273.

After the failure of her marriage to her first husband, she settled into her renewed sense of purpose. This courageous woman was not just satisfied with winning her freedom.

She went back into slave-driven areas to be the light for so many enslaved people. She was a woman full of conviction who trusted The Redeemer to lead her throughout all the seasons of her life.

"The four phases of Tubman's life—a slave; an abolitionist and conductor on the Underground Railroad; a Civil War soldier, nurse, spy and scout; and a social reformer—are important aspects of her dedication to service." [14]

It is important to remember that she could not have reached freedom without some help along the way. Cleveland was a major stop on the Underground Railroad. "Known by its code name of 'Hope,' runaway slaves knew that once they had crossed the Ohio River, traveled through Ripley and reached Cleveland, they were steps closer to freedom. The Cozad-Bates House was owned by a wealthy abolitionist family who stowed runaways. St. John's Episcopal Church was the last stop on the Underground Railroad before runaway slaves took a boat across Lake Erie into Canada."[15]

Wonderful people of all backgrounds sympathized with the plight along with Harriet. Some hid runaway slaves in their businesses and homes. Others provided food and clothing. Freedom was the cause for which they were fighting.

Just like Harriet, I learned that I could not be a good resource to others unless I grieved my own losses and then moved onward.

Today, there is a fundamental failure to listen internally and to each other. We live in strange times of exhaustion from information overload. Prideful rhetoric and influencers promote multiple products. It is harder and harder to manage information daily. Social media, webpages, mobile apps, and emails compete for our daily responses. There is a political exploitation of emotions and the pressure to respond adds to our information overload.

Can these same platforms, which may be beneficial to good organizations and businesses to share necessary information, also be stirring the proverbial pot of political and racial unrest? We are too easily distracted from ourselves and are no longer paying attention to that still small voice on the inside.

---

[14] .Christianity Today, Harriet Tubman- The "Moses" of her People, Christian History
https://www.christianitytoday.com/history/people/activists/harriet-tubman.html

[15] Lewis, Femi. "Five Cities of the Abolition Movement." ThoughtCo, Feb. 11, 2020, thoughtco.com/five-cities-of-the-abolition-movement-45413.

Let's be counter-cultural by being intentional about accessing the power of hope.

1. Pick one day to focus on gratitude.
   Dedicate it fully to staying mindful of the blessings given to you. My day is Friday. Write in your journal the parts of your life for which you are most thankful. Share your grateful spirit with someone who is in a dark spot. Tell someone that you are thankful for their presence during the dark times of your life. In prayer, do not ask for anything. Opt for blessing the Lord with your praises and awareness of His goodness in your life. On this set-apart day, listen to others witness their struggles and griefs. God has blessed you in some way, give it back by being present in someone else's pain. Make sure that you do not over-function as a "Band-aid applier" but hear what is in their heart. You will be prompted to respond if more is necessary.

2. Increase Faith in God daily.
   Avoid faith in faith itself. I caution against this because it is humanistic and thus is void of lasting power. Romans 10:17 states, *"So then faith comes by hearing, and hearing by the word of God."* The word of God is purifying to the mind so focus on God to heal your thoughts. Confess your prideful or resentful thoughts. Set your mind to higher things.

   What thoughts do you need to submit to God? Our minds can be hostile to God. I love to read the Bible but listening also commits it to memory. Listen to a form of the Word daily. The Bible App YouVersion offers a free Bible experience for tablets, smartphones and online at Bible.com. So does BibleGateway.com.

   Ask God to heal your thoughts that are contrary to the word of God? Share what you have learned about God's Word.

3. Lean into Hope.
   Sometimes what you hope for will come about as expected. Hebrews 11:1 declares that *"faith is the substance of things hoped for the evidence of things not seen."*

   Sometimes what you hope for will not happen. What do you do when faith disappoints? Or your life does not turn out as expected? Does it mean that God is not faithful?

   No, it means that life is hard. Some of us have been sold on the unrealistic truth that God gives us exactly what we want, or when we want it like a heavenly Santa Claus. This is the reason why people have fallen away from faith in God. They say faith did not "work for them." I exhort you, to lean in. Lean into Hope.

The Word of God is sharp and powerful (Hebrews 4:12). That is why the previous step of increasing your faith daily by studying the Word is crucial. Faith will produce a harvest of peace and joy. The Word of God is life and it births a hope that cannot be denied. A hope that stirs up all the possibilities for a future never imagined.

When you lean into hope, you experience the exhilaration of The Redeemer working on your behalf. It is glorious to be a kept woman. Kept in his care. Kept in his love. He will redeem all things. Trust in it.

As you go through the RECOVER Me healing and recovery process, write down in your journal meditation scripture verses that highlight hope. One that I would meditate on is found in Romans 5:5, *"Now hope does not disappoint, because the love of God has been poured out in our hearts by the Holy Spirit who was given to us."*

Switch them out once you gained some revelation of those Scripture verses and have memorized and internalized them. Choose new scriptures as often as needed. *"Let the words of mouth, and the meditations of my heart, be acceptable in thy sight, Oh Lord, my strength and my Redeemer."* Psalm 19:14

4. Let Hope Inform Your Decisions
   There are risks in life. Risks in starting a business, being alone, or being in community. There are also rewards that show up to light your path. If you lean into hope, endings can guide you to new beginnings. Maybe not the new beginnings that you hoped for or expected, but even more fulfilling if you give it a chance.

   In your journal, share your relationship with hope. Go deeper, reflecting on some new beginnings being birthed in your life today. Is some residual anger, lack of closure, or forgiveness standing in your way? Pray on it for several weeks.

   Share your process or stuck points with a trusted mentor. Pray together with that mentor, asking for the release of anger and the freedom that is found in forgiveness. Forgiveness allows you to detach peacefully from past hurts. Forgiveness is often a process involving prayer and truthful acceptance. Forgive me for my trespasses as we forgive those who trespass against us.

5. Find Community on Purpose

Life is done better together. "In this respect, just as secure attachment to parents instills hope in children, secures attachment to God and to groups can foster hope in adults. "[16]

You learn from each other and inspire one another to reflect and to act. It is important to seek social engagement, especially in times of crisis. The sense of community and connection in a group where there is a shared goal is of the utmost importance. There is an old saying that Satan divides, but God unites. Do not feel you have to go it alone, ever.

The goal may be recreational, community service-orientated, or a recovery of some sort. Your church or fellowship may have some volunteer opportunities and ministries that you can get involved in. Stay committed to it for a set time, at least three to six months. There is healing in consistency and power in belonging. Many people forfeit productive lives due to the lack of commitment and are confused when a lack of peace is the outcome of their isolation.

Hope will not leave me alone because miracles do happen. I believe that more now than ever. I have seen seemingly impossible situations improve. I have seen God's love lavishly bless people, including myself.

The beauty of a crisis of any kind is that it can lead to necessary detachment. That was my journey. My dreams are now born of God. His unexpected blessings humbled me leaving me wanting more of his divine will for my life..

Hope has set me on another path that I am curious about exploring. I am embracing new opportunities. I enjoy recovering a new sense of purpose. This purpose is birthed out of pain of my physical barrenness. This purpose leads me to create solutions to problems that I feel called to solve- a new birthing of sorts. I am now choosing to fully engage in the next part of my life's journey. I cannot wait to see the life that God has planned me.

Walking through infertility has taught me to be vulnerable. In my weakness, Jesus strengthened me through my connection to Him that says, *"My yoke is easy, and my burden is light"* (Matthew 11:30.)

The redemption comes through making Jesus my number one attachment. Other attachments are crucial, but only One sustains. He will continue to lead my paths. How do I not get lost in the hard stuff? The answer is to lose myself in the will of Jesus.

I am not pursuing perfection, but His presence. *"Whoever finds his life will lose it, and whoever loses his life for my sake will find it"* (Matthew 10:9, see also Mark 8:35, Luke 9:24, John 12:25.)

He continues to restore my body, my soul, and my spirit.

---

[16] Shorey, Snyder, Yang, & Lewin, 2003

Welcoming Rest

Sit in a comfortable position.
Breathe in through your nose.
Let your belly fill with air.
Breathe out through your nose.
Place one hand on your heart.
Pay attention to your breathing.
Breathe normally.
Reflections on your journey
See my heart, Lord.
Lost things and hopes unfulfilled
Can I trust you with broken things, God?
Faith
Free me from any anger, sadness, and shame trapped inside of me.
Help me to see my heart as it is human.
I accept the invitation to follow you.
Yoke me to you.
Hope
Heal my heart.
Reflections of your journey
Breathe in through your nose.
Let your belly fill with air.
Breathe out through your nose.
Pay attention to your breathing.
Breathe in His way.
Breathe out Fear.
Redeemer's Love.
Recover Me.

Continue this section with a one-hour Heart Meditation on ABIDE.

HEALING YOUR HEART FROM TROUBLE Meditation GUIDE - Feel God's Healing Hands & Heal while You Sleep. You can download the ABIDE app, visit the website at https://abide.co/ or sample it on YouTube.

Prayer Matters

The Redeemer of all things teaches us the way to pray in Matthew 6:9-13. Let these words ground you in His care.

Our Father, who art in heaven,
hallowed be thy name;
thy kingdom come;
thy will be done;
on earth as it is in heaven.
Give us this day our daily bread.
And forgive us our trespasses,
as we forgive those who trespass against us.
And lead us not into temptation,
but deliver us from evil.
For thine is the kingdom,
the power and the glory,
for ever and ever.
Amen.

Acknowledgements

I wish to express my sincere appreciation for this book project:

Julie B. Cosgrove, my content editor, for helping me to frame the book, sharing your writing expertise, and for your commitment to bringing out the best in me.

Freda Nettleton, my special proofing editor, for your wisdom, commitment, and generous support.

Dr. Mark McKinney, for paving the way through pastoral counseling education with a special emphasis on self-awareness and self-care. You did this way before it was popular.

Celeste Wells, Susan Johnson, Tywanna Johnson, Annie Smith, and Sue Farrell, who have been my inspirations. Thank you for your attention to detail, vision, and life-giving words during the birth of this book.

To the first Group Facilitators, Cynthia Ann Guastaferri, Sacha Nichole Warrum and Carrie Waug. Thank you for your belief in RECOVER Me in its earliest stages. Your faith and works are true gifts.

To the Calvary Life Senior Pastors, John and Carmela Muratori, for your commitment to the call, the Word of God and for releasing us to plant the Calvary Life DFW campus.

To the Calvary Life DFW Associate Pastors, Steve and Leona Bontrager, for sharing friendship, unity and passion of sound doctrine with us.

To my father, Kenneth Driffin, you taught me the power of the spoken word. I am forever grateful.

To my Grandmothers, Elizabeth Tanner and Mary Driffin, my Aunts Lois Tanner-Baker and the late Velver Brown, for your examples of hard work, perseverance, and setting your children's children up for success.

To Connie (Judah), Tiffani (Rodney), Brittani, Aleesha, Tae, and Brandon. Thank you for loving me and accepting me into the Fraser Camp.

To my mother and my confidant, Rose Tanner-Elzey (Marvin). You were my true inspiration for this book. Your lifestyle of obedience to God and pure joy are matchless.

And finally, to the best husband in the world, Gwynmar Fraser, for your unwavering integrity and keen emotional intelligence. Your gentle guidance and kindness make it a pleasure to be covered by you.

Above all else, I praise our Lord, Jesus Christ, for His unwavering love for us all, His healing power in our lives, and His gracious mercy. I pray this work honors Him and that He will use it to His glory.

Yolanda Fraser, LCSW

Final Notes:

Appendix

RECOVER Me Support Groups

RECOVER Me is a navigation tool to help you move through your journey. Some women prefer to join a RECOVER Me support group. Our RECOVER Me support groups typically meet in churches or faith-based locations. Virtual groups are another option. Please visit our website at www.recovermesupport.com to learn about RECOVER Me groups, resources or becoming a RM Facilitator.

Support Group Sessions

RECOVER Me groups are eight weeks long. They are led by RM Group Leaders who receive training and ongoing group training

Week 1- Introduction to the RECOVER Me journey

Week 2- Roles of Attachment

Week 3- Empathize with Your Experiences

Week 4- Come to Your Safe Place

Week 5- Open Your Heart to New Ways of Being

Week 6- Voice Your Boundaries

Week 7- Explore Your Purpose

Week 8- Remember the Power of Hope

RECOVER Me is a support group. This is not a professional counseling group. Your RM Facilitator can direct you to sources for professional and/or pastoral counseling.

RM Facilitator will start each group with the reading of the group guidelines.

1. I agree that everything stated in this group must remain confidential.
2. I have the right not to share.
3. I share my own experiences, using "I" statements when sharing.
4. I will abstain from giving advice, allowing others to experience their own process of recovery and feelings.
5. I am respectful of the time, sharing for three to five minutes.

RM Facilitator has the great responsibility of managing the content and safety of the group. They have the right to redirect group participants to ensure the integrity of the group.

Structure of the RECOVER ME Support Group

1. Group Rules
2. RM Facilitator introduces a new recovery skill.
3. Group Participants will reflect, and answer questions related to recovery skill.
4. Closing Meditation and Prayer Matters

Made in the USA
Middletown, DE
18 September 2020